Phonics and Spelling
3

Julie Crimmins-Crocker

Acknowledgements

© 2007 Folens Limited, on behalf of the author.

UK: Folens Publishers, Apex Business Centre, Boscombe Road, Dunstable, LU5 4RL.
www.folens.com

Ireland: Folens Publishers, Greenhills Road, Tallaght, Dublin 24.

Managing editor: Joanne Mitchell
Editor: Charlie Wilson
Layout artist: Neil Hawkins, ndesign
Illustrations: JB Illustrations, Nicola Pearce and Sarah Wade at SGA and Leonie Shearing c/o Lucas Alexander Whitley.
Cover design: Blayney Partnership

First published 2007 by Folens Limited.

Every effort has been made to contact copyright holders of material used in this publication. If any copyright holder has been overlooked, we should be pleased to make any necessary arrangements.

British Library Cataloguing in Publication Data. A catalogue record for this publication is available from the British Library.

ISBN 978-1-85008-240-8

Contents

This contents list provides an overview of the learning objectives of each puzzle page.

Tips for teachers

Practise with Puzzles can be used alongside any existing phonics programme. Use the puzzles to:

- provide extension activities;
- provide homework tasks;
- reinforce or revise spelling patterns covered in a lesson;
- provide extra practice for less able children;
- provide a challenge for more able children.

Here are some ideas to make the puzzle sessions more enjoyable and successful:

- First, introduce the children to the concept covered in the puzzle, then read through the word bank together. The word banks can be omitted when photocopying to make the puzzles more challenging.

- Read through the 'How to complete the puzzles' (see page 4) with the children or photocopy this sheet for them to refer to.

- Provide additional support for children by filling in letters or more challenging words, prior to photocopying.

- After completion of the puzzle, introduce the children to 'What's next?' (see page 5), which outlines valuable reinforcement and extension activities. These can be linked to any puzzle page.

- 'What's next?' can also be photocopied for children to refer to and provides a personal record of the activities they have completed.

How to complete the puzzles

 Read the title and the instructions for each activity very carefully.

 For each activity, start with the simplest clues first.

 Crossword and wordsearch clues have numbers at the end of each clue to tell you how many letters there are in the word.

 If there is a word bank for you to refer to, check that your answers are in the list. Cross out the words in the word bank as you complete the clue.

 Use a sharp pencil at first to write down all your answers (just in case you need to change them).

 When you are sure your answers are correct, write them in pen or use a highlighter pen for the wordsearches.

 In the crosswords, write in CAPITAL LETTERS. This will make your answers easier to read.

 Use a dictionary and thesaurus to help you spell and find your answers.

Remember what these useful words mean:

Synonym: the same or similar meaning, for example, *big – large*.

Antonym: the opposite meaning, for example, *big – small*.

Anagram: the word is muddled up, for example, *GREAL – LARGE*.

Informal: the word is simple or slang, for example, *rabbit – bunny*.

Verbs are action and 'doing' words, for example, *run*, *talk* and *think*.

Nouns are naming words, for example, *pen*, *hat*, *apple* and *school*.

Adjectives are describing words, for example, *small* bird.

Adverbs add more information to verbs, for example, He ran *quickly*.

Phoneme: a letter or letters that when said aloud create a single sound, for example, **TH** and **OO**.

Letter string: a collection of phonemes, for example, **ELL**.

Vowels are the letters **a**, **e**, **i**, **o** and **u**.

Consonants are the letters of the alphabet which are <u>not</u> vowels.

Most importantly, ENJOY YOURSELF!

What's next?

Use the answers to any of the puzzles to complete the following activities. Write down which activity you have completed and the date you did it.

	Activity	Puzzle title	Date
★1	Sort the answers into **alphabetical order**. Put them in a list.		
★2	Put the answers into **sentences** (10 sentences minimum). You can use one word per sentence or include as many words as you like in each sentence.		
★3	Put the answers into sentences that are questions. For example, *Where did my cat go?*		
★4	Put the answers into sentences that are instructions. For example, *Look after my cat when I am away.*		
★5	Put the words in the word bank into a story or piece of writing.		
★6	Write at least ten more of the same type of word.		
★7	Find **synonyms** for the words and write them down in pairs or groups. For example, *big – large, massive.*		
★8	Find **antonyms** for the words and write them down in pairs or groups. For example, *big – small, tiny, minute.*		
★9	Find **rhymes** for the words and list them. For example, *ink – sink* and *bellow – yellow, mellow* and *fellow.*		
★10	Sort the answers into groups (as instructed by your teacher). For example, verbs, nouns, adjectives, adverbs, number of syllables, rhyming words and so on.		
★11	Write your own new clues for the answers to a crossword, wordsearch or puzzle or create a totally new puzzle.		

Alphabetical order

In a dictionary words are listed in alphabetical order from A to Z. In the spaceship there are different foods. Sort them into alphabetical order and write them on the shopping list. Look at the first phoneme of each word. Two items have been written in for you.

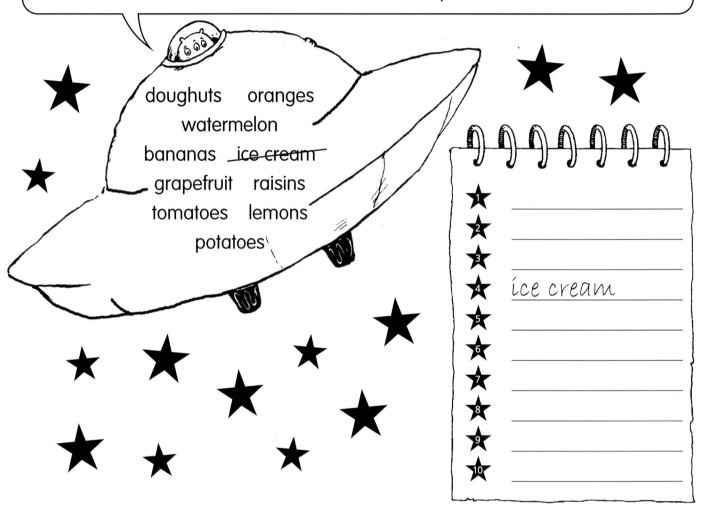

doughuts   oranges
watermelon
bananas   ice cream
grapefruit   raisins
tomatoes   lemons
potatoes

1
2
3
4 ice cream
5
6
7
8
9
10

Write the first phoneme to complete the words. Then sort the words into alphabetical order on the lines below.

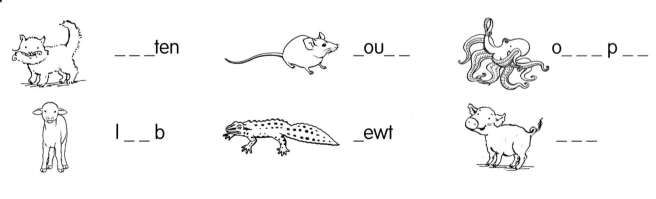

_ _ _ten

_ou_ _

o_ _ _ p _ _

l _ _ b

_ewt

_ _ _

Alphabetical order

The words in the table are listed in alphabetical order but their letters are all muddled up. Finish writing the alphabet first, then unjumble the letters and write the words on the lines. The first one has been done for you. Use the word bank to help you.

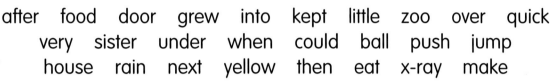

Word bank

after   food   door   grew   into   kept   little   zoo   over   quick
very   sister   under   when   could   ball   push   jump
house   rain   next   yellow   then   eat   x-ray   make

★	rafte	a	after	★14	texn		
★2	lalb	b		★15	revo		
★3	dulco	c		★16	shup		
★4	rodo			★17	uckiq		
★5	tea			★18	nira		
★6	fodo			★19	tessir		
★7	werg			★20	neth		
★8	eshou			★21	redun		
★9	toni			★22	yvre		
★10	pumj			★23	henw		
★11	petk			★24	r-axy		
★12	tillet			★25	welloy		
★13	keam			★26	ozo		

Sort these nouns into alphabetical order.

rabbit   prince   fish   igloo   apple   door   lamp   zip   whale   umbrella

Phonics and Spelling 3

Syllables

Words are made up of syllables. Syllables are parts of words, for example, *sun* has one syllable, *Sunday* has two (**Sun** + **day**) and *Saturday* has three (**Sat** + **ur** + **day**). Saying the separate syllables in words can help you read, write and spell them correctly.

Join these syllables together to make words. Write the words on the lines.

★1 aft + er = _____after_____   ★6 broth + er = _____

★2 ver + y = _____   ★7 Tues + day = _____

★3 Sat + ur + day = _____   ★8 Dec + em + ber = _____

★4 be + fore = _____   ★9 to + night = _____

★5 morn + ing = _____   ★10 kitt + en = _____

Divide these words into their separate syllables.

★1 flower   = ___flow___ + ___er___   ★6 today   = _____ + _____

★2 Friday   = _____ + _____   ★7 begin   = _____ + _____

★3 sister   = _____ + _____   ★8 July   = _____ + _____

★4 yellow   = _____ + _____   ★9 twenty   = _____ + _____

★5 nineteen = _____ + _____   ★10 going   = _____ + _____

Syllables

Write the rocket words in the syllable planets according to the number of syllables they have.

very

time

brother

them

over

Monday

school

could

water

Words with one syllable

boy

Words with two syllables

Cross out the words with more than one syllable in the lists below. Write the one-syllable words that are left on the line below to discover the hidden sentence.

At sister about school I because learn how never to teacher read and spell happy

I another learn into how to only draw flower and count father too

High frequency words

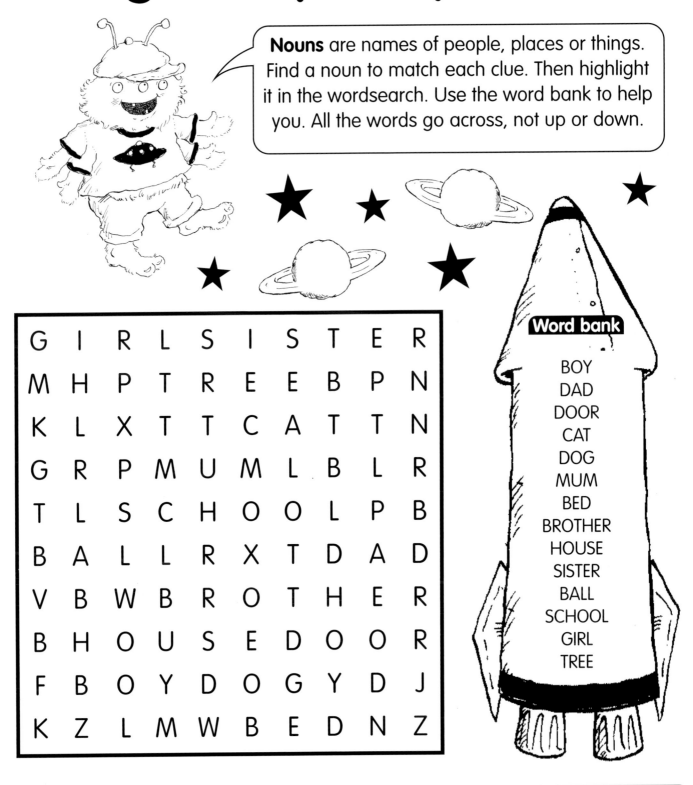

Nouns are names of people, places or things. Find a noun to match each clue. Then highlight it in the wordsearch. Use the word bank to help you. All the words go across, not up or down.

G	I	R	L	S	I	S	T	E	R
M	H	P	T	R	E	E	B	P	N
K	L	X	T	T	C	A	T	T	N
G	R	P	M	U	M	L	B	L	R
T	L	S	C	H	O	O	L	P	B
B	A	L	L	R	X	T	D	A	D
V	B	W	B	R	O	T	H	E	R
B	H	O	U	S	E	D	O	O	R
F	B	O	Y	D	O	G	Y	D	J
K	Z	L	M	W	B	E	D	N	Z

Word bank

BOY
DAD
DOOR
CAT
DOG
MUM
BED
BROTHER
HOUSE
SISTER
BALL
SCHOOL
GIRL
TREE

1. A building you can live in (5)   **2.** A short word for father (3)   **3.** An animal that purrs (3)   **4.** You sleep in this (3)   **5.** An antonym for girl (3)   **6.** An animal that barks (3)   **7.** A short word for mother (3)   **8.** You open this to go into a room (4)   **9.** You can play games like tennis and rugby with this (4)   **10.** A place where teachers work (6)   **11.** This big plant has a trunk and leaves (4)   **12.** An antonym for boy (4)   **13.** A boy with the same mum and dad as another (7)
14. A girl with the same mum and dad as another (6)

Phonics and Spelling 3

High frequency words

Verbs are doing words that tell you what someone or something is doing. Find the verb in the word bank for each clue and write it in the crossword in capital letters.

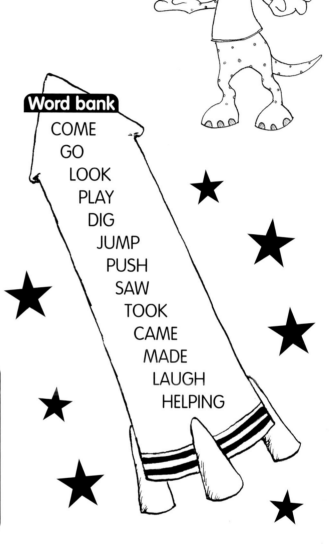

Word bank
- COME
- GO
- LOOK
- PLAY
- DIG
- JUMP
- PUSH
- SAW
- TOOK
- CAME
- MADE
- LAUGH
- HELPING

ACROSS
3. You use your eyes to do this (4)
5. An antonym for go (4)
6. A frog can do this and so can a flea (4)
8. An antonym for pull (4)
11. You do this with a spade (3)
12. The past tense of come (4)

DOWN
1. An antonym for come (2)
2. The past tense of take (4)
3. You do this if something is funny (5)
4. Kind people like _ _ _ _ _ _ _ others (7)
7. It is nice to _ _ _ _ in the park (4)
9. The past tense of make (4)
10. The past tense of see (3)

Short A phoneme

These words have a short **A** phoneme, for example, *bag* and *pack*. Add the first phoneme to these words. Some have pictures and some have clues to help you.

1. [___ap]
2. Carry shopping in this [___ag]
3. Wave this for your country [___lag]
4. Unhappy [___ad]
5. Not good [___ad]

6. [___at]
7. The past tense of have [___ad]
8. Another word for happy [___lad]
9. The past tense of run [___an]
10. Wear this on your head [___at]

Join a phoneme or blend to the rest of the word and write it on the line. One has been done for you.

1st syllable	2nd syllable	Complete word
st	atch	
f	ad	
m	at	
gl	ack	
bl	amp	stamp
cl	and	
l	an	
h	ab	
pl	amp	
gr	amb	

Circle the short **A** phoneme in these words.

1. animal 2. planet 3. ragdoll 4. milkman 5. teabag

6. kneecap 7. fatter 8. clapping 9. capital 10. trapdoor

Phonics and Spelling 3

Short E phoneme

These words have a short **E** phoneme, for example, *vet* and *them*. Add the first phoneme to these words. Some have pictures and some have clues to help you.

1. [__ed]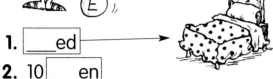

2. 10 [__en]

3. North, South, East and [__est]

4. [__en]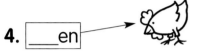

5. A bird lays eggs in this [__est]

6. [__eg]

7. This goes 'ding dong' [__ell]

8. An antonym for buy [__ell]

9. [__et]

10. The plural of man [__en]

Circle the short **E** phoneme in the rockets.

Join a phoneme or blend to the rest of the word and write it on the line. One has been done for you.

1st syllable	2nd syllable	Complete word
f	ed	
dr	ep	
st	est	
t	ess	
r	ence	*fence*
b	ept	
n	em	
k	edge	
th	ext	
h	est	

1. blackberry

2. address

3. yellow

4. bedroom

5. kettle

6. princess

7. better

8. cherry

9. petal

10. exit

Short I phoneme

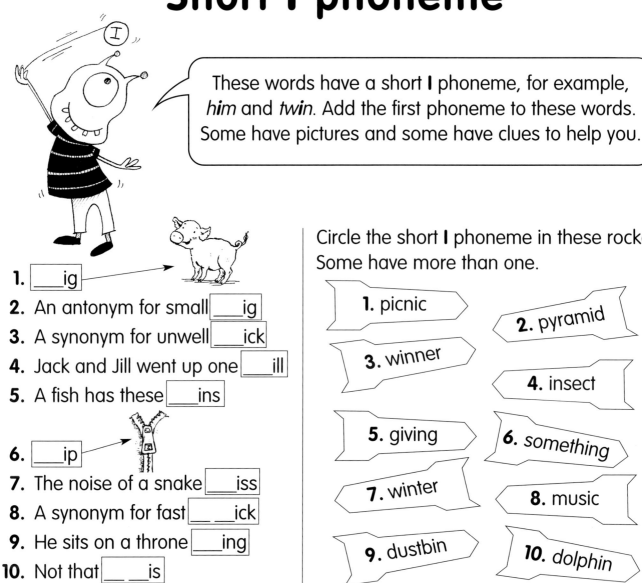

These words have a short **I** phoneme, for example, *him* and *twin*. Add the first phoneme to these words. Some have pictures and some have clues to help you.

1. ___ig
2. An antonym for small ___ig
3. A synonym for unwell ___ick
4. Jack and Jill went up one ___ill
5. A fish has these ___ins
6. ___ip
7. The noise of a snake ___iss
8. A synonym for fast ___ ___ick
9. He sits on a throne ___ing
10. Not that ___ ___is

Circle the short **I** phoneme in these rockets. Some have more than one.

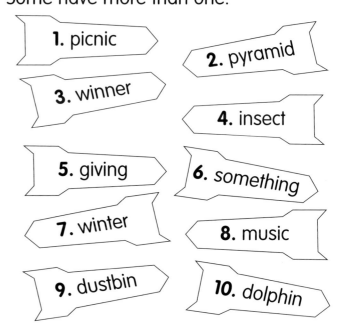

1. picnic
2. pyramid
3. winner
4. insect
5. giving
6. something
7. winter
8. music
9. dustbin
10. dolphin

Join a phoneme or blend to the rest of the word and write it on the line. One has been done for you.

1st syllable	2nd syllable	Complete word
tw	in	
sw	id	
th	ink	
dr	im	
k	ig	twig
sw	im	
pr	iff	
sn	itch	
spr	ip	
sk	ing	

Phonics and Spelling 3

Short O phoneme

These words have a short **O** phoneme, for example, *not* and *lost*. Add the first phoneme to these words. Some have pictures and some have clues to help you.

1. [___og]
2. To jump on one leg [___op]
3. An antonym for cold [___ot]
4. Used to clean floors [___op]
5. Not hard [___oft]

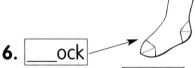

6. [___ock]
7. A big stone [___ock]
8. A burst balloon goes [___op]
9. Like a toad [___rog]
10. Where fish swim in a garden [___ond]

Circle the short **O** phoneme in these words. Some may have more than one.

1. unlock
2. bottom
3. proper
4. hedgehog
5. forgot
9. toffee
6. rotten
7. oblong
8. ping-pong
10. lollipop

Join a phoneme or blend to the rest of the word and write it on the lines. One has been done for you.

1st syllable	2nd syllable	Complete word
st	ost	
c	oss	
cr	ock	
l	ob	
i	op	stop
b	op	
t	ob	
cl	oss	
str	ong	
r	ock	

Short U phoneme

These words have a short **U** phoneme, for example, *club* and *flush*.

Circle the short **U** phoneme in these words. Some may have more than one.

1. buttercup
2. grumpy
3. buckle
4. unlucky
5. bucket
6. hiccup
7. puppies
8. bubble
9. dummy
10. chipmunk

Add the first phoneme to these words. Some have pictures and some have clues to help you.

1. ___rum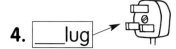
2. Another word for an insect ___ug
3. The past tense of stick ___tuck
4. ___lug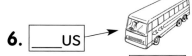
5. A short word for mother ___um
6. ___us
7. A large cup ___ug
8. Another word for and ___lus
9. Use it to tidy hair ___rush
10. Useless rubbish ___unk

Join a phoneme or blend to the rest of the word and write it on the line. One has been done for you.

1st syllable	2nd syllable	Complete word
tr	ut	
sh	ub	
cl	ump	
h	unt	
j	unk	trunk
t	uch	
s	usk	
gl	ust	
h	um	
cr	utch	

Various short vowel phonemes

These words have short vowel phonemes, **A, E, I, O** or **U**, for example, *bag, beg, big, dog* and *dug*. Find the answers to the clues and write them in the crossword in capital letters. Use the word bank to help you.

Word bank

SHIP
SNAP
NUTS
GRIN
KNOT
LEGS
BOTTOM
CHIN
PLANET
CHIPS
PENCILS
PINS
UP
TRUNK
CATFLAP
JAM
BERRIES
UPON

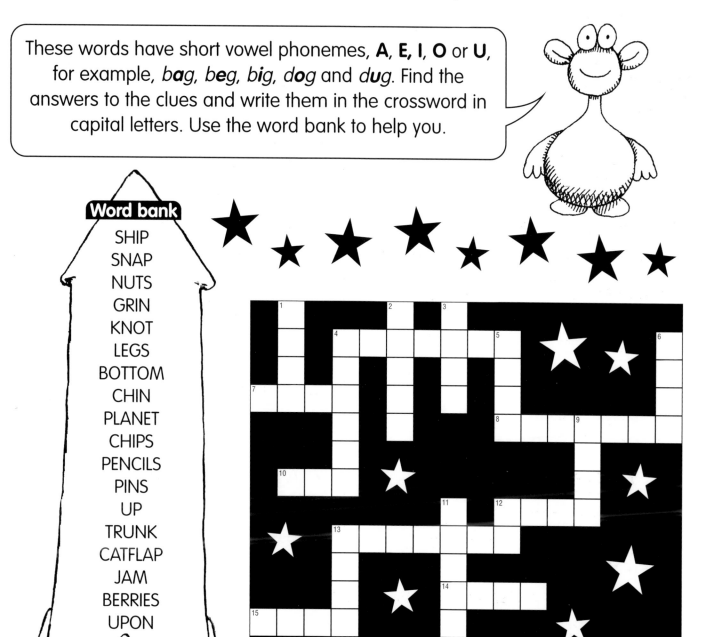

ACROSS

4. Small fruits (7)   **7.** Tie this in a shoelace (4)   **8.** Use these to draw (7)   **10.** A fruity spread (3)   **12.** Stories sometimes start 'Once _ _ _ _ a time' (4)   **13.** A small door for a cat (7)   **14.** Squirrels eat these (4)   **15.** A simple card game (4)

DOWN

1. A big smile (4)   **2.** Part of a tree (5)   **3.** Use these when sewing (4)   **4.** Not the top (6)   **5.** A large boat (4)   **6.** A dog has four of these (4)   **9.** Where a beard grows (4)   **11.** Mars is one (6)   **12.** The opposite of down (2)   **13.** Fried potatoes eaten with fish (5)

Phonics and Spelling 3

Silent E

These words all end with a silent **E** which makes the vowel sound long, for example, *mad – made*, *pip – pipe*, *hop – hope* and *cub – cube*. Solve the clues and find the answers in the wordsearch. The words can only be read across and down, not diagonally.

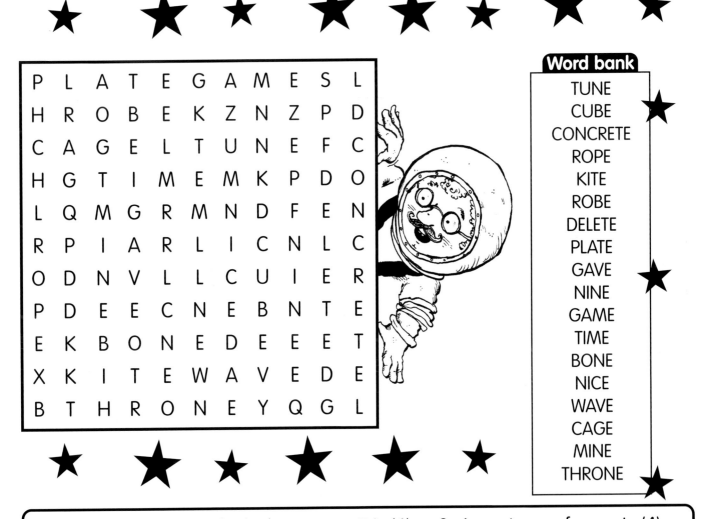

P	L	A	T	E	G	A	M	E	S	L
H	R	O	B	E	K	Z	N	Z	P	D
C	A	G	E	L	T	U	N	E	F	C
H	G	T	I	M	E	M	K	P	D	O
L	Q	M	G	R	M	N	D	F	E	N
R	P	I	A	R	L	I	C	N	L	C
O	D	N	V	L	L	C	U	I	E	R
P	D	E	E	C	N	E	B	N	T	E
E	K	B	O	N	E	D	E	E	E	T
X	K	I	T	E	W	A	V	E	D	E
B	T	H	R	O	N	E	Y	Q	G	L

Word bank

TUNE
CUBE
CONCRETE
ROPE
KITE
ROBE
DELETE
PLATE
GAVE
NINE
GAME
TIME
BONE
NICE
WAVE
CAGE
MINE
THRONE

1. A clock will help you find what _ _ _ _ it is (4)   **2.** An antonym for nasty (4)
3. A _ _ _ _ _ makes the sea move (4)   **4.** That is not yours it is _ _ _ _ (4)
5. An elegant long flowing coat (4)   **6.** The past tense of give (4)   **7.** A king sits on this (6)   **8.** Five plus four equals this (4)   **9.** Something you play (4)
10. Like string, but thicker and stronger (4)   **11.** Dogs like to chew on this (4)
12. A six-faced 3-D shape (4)   **13.** A song has words and a _ _ _ _ (4)   **14.** To rub out or get rid of (6)   **15.** To make a wall you need bricks and this (8)
16. You can fly this diamond shape (4)   **17.** My hamster lives in one (4)
18. We eat food on one (5)

Phonics and Spelling 3

Long I with GHT

The letter string **IGHT** has a long **I** phoneme, for example, *light* and *fight*. This phoneme can also be spelt **ITE** with a silent **E**, for example, *kite* and *bite*.

Circle the words with the long **I** phoneme (**ITE** or **IGHT**).

fight	first	sit
night	list	bright
bite	sight	white
fist	fit	milk

Circle the long **I** phoneme in these words.

1. lightning   **2.** excited   **3.** midnight   **4.** moonlight   **5.** polite

Find the answers to the clues below, then write the letters in the word boxes. The shape of the boxes will help you work out what type of letter goes inside it.

tight
knight
midnight
tonight
right

Example

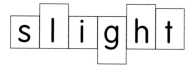

1. Not loose

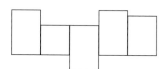

2. This evening

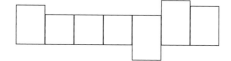

4. 12 o'clock at night

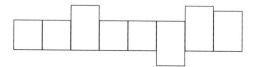

3. He wears armour and rides a horse

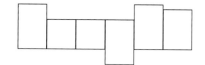

5. Correct, not wrong

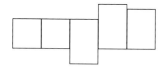

Phonics and Spelling 3

Long A phoneme

The answers to the puzzles on this page have a long **A** phoneme. This phoneme can be spelt three ways:
- **A** + silent **E** as in *cake*
- **AI** as in *rain*
- **AY** as in *way*.

Circle the words with a long **A** phoneme and write them in the correct column in the table.

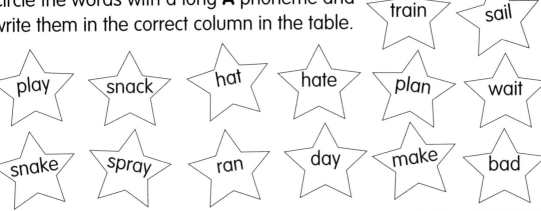

train   sail

play   snack   hat   hate   plan   wait

snake   spray   ran   day   make   bad

A + silent E	AI	AY

Write the answers to the clues in capital letters in the stepword. Some letters have been written in to help you.

1. S P C
3. S L
5. M D
   R
7. N M
   N

1. Where the stars and planets are
2. We eat these on our birthdays
3. A boat catches the wind in this
4. A match will make one of these
5. The past tense of make
6. Water runs down this
7. What you are called is your _ _ _ _
8. The fur around a lion's face

Phonics and Spelling 3

Long A phoneme

Fill in the missing letters in the A frames. In each A frame you will find three words and the three different ways of spelling the long **A** phoneme. Use the word bank to help you.

Word bank

nails	days	train	snake	snail	hay
stay	case	rain	ape	ace	May

1. The number one playing card

2. There are seven of these in a week

3. A slow garden pest

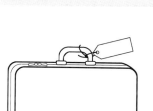

4. The month before June

5. You pack this for a holiday

6. Makes a 'choo choo' sound

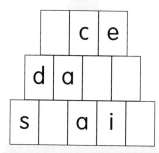

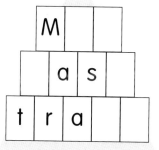

7. A monkey with no tail

8. An antonym for go

9. You can hit these in with a hammer

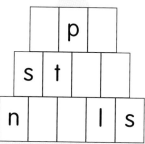

10. Dried grass for farm animals to eat

11. Water that falls from the sky

12. A slippery, long creature

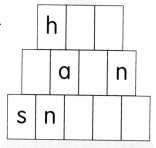

Long E phoneme

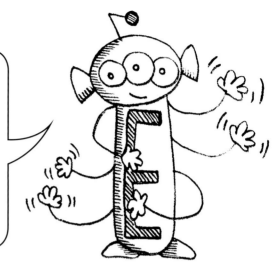

The answers to these puzzles have a long **E** phoneme. This phoneme can be spelt four ways:
- **EE** as in *see*
- **EA** as in *cream*
- **E** as in *me*
- **E** + silent **E** as in *here*.

Circle the words with a long **E** phoneme and write them in the table.

net   queen   each   bed   we   test   be

EE	EA	E

green   clear   help   went   meat   he   keep

Circle the long **E** phoneme in these words, for example, te(a)spoon.

teacher   weekend   sixteen   before   sunbeam   eating   teabag

★ ★

Look at the letter strings in the rockets and rearrange them to make six words with a long **E** phoneme.

1. ee ch se   **2.** ea dr m   **3.** ee scr n

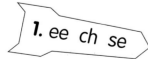**4.** sp d ee   **5.** pe stam de   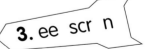**6.** n ea m

Long E phoneme

Solve the clues to fill in the missing letters in each **E** frame. Use the word bank to help you.

1. The colour of leaves

2. I love my mum, _ _ _ is kind

3. An antonym for dirty

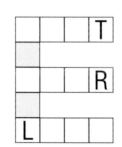

4. We walk on these

5. 12 months

6. This grows on a tree

7. You do this in bed

8. Small round green vegetables

9. Two plus one equals this

10. We get wool from these animals

11. Birds have these

12. To take something that isn't yours

Long I phoneme

The answers to these puzzles have the long **I** phoneme. This phoneme can be spelt four ways:
- **I** + silent **E** as in *like*
- **IE** as in *flies*
- **IGH**T as in *flight*
- **Y** as in *sky* (**Y** only has a long **I** phoneme in one-syllable words).

Circle the words with a long **I** phoneme and write them in the table.

I + silent E	Y	IE	IGH

Circle the long **I** phoneme in these words, for example, sunl**igh**t.

bedtime   inside   beehive   tonight   surprise   midnight   polite   pantomime

Circle the correct spelling for these words.

★1	fite	fight	fiet
★2	bite	bight	biet
★3	spise	spies	spys
★4	fire	fyre	fier
★5	mice	myce	miec
★6	dry	drie	drigh

Long I phoneme

Solve the clues to fill in the missing letters in the crosswords. In each crossword frame you will find two different spellings for the long **I** phoneme. Use the word bank to help you.

1. Not loose
2. Eight plus one equals this

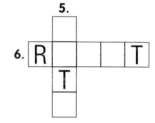

Word bank

SKY	FIVE
NINE	WHITE
KNIGHT	MICE
KITE	RIGHT
LIGHT	BIKE
PIES	TIGHT

3. Three plus two equals this
4. Santa enjoys mince _ _ _ _

5. You fly this diamond shape
6. An antonym for left

7. The colour of snow
8. He wears armour and rides a horse

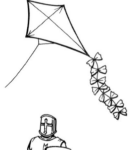

9. A short word for a bicycle
10. Where the clouds are

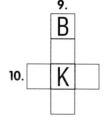

11. Not heavy or dark
12. Three blind _ _ _ _

Long O phoneme

The answers to these puzzles have the long **O** phoneme. This phoneme can be spelt five ways:
- **O** + silent **E** as in *close*
- **OA** as in *road*
- **OE** as in *toe*
- **O** as in *so*
- **OW** as in *snow*.

Circle the words with a long **O** phoneme and write those words in the table.

home   joke   off   hot   goes   road
lost
song   shop   toes   no   show
go   coal   know

O + silent E	OA	OE	O	OW

Circle the long **O** phoneme in these words, for example, hell(o).

hose   October   window   yellow   video   shadow

explode   elbow   tiptoe

Circle the correct spelling for these words.

★1	bote	boat	bowt
★2	note	noat	noet
★3	windoe	windo	window
★4	pianoe	piano	pianow
★5	toest	toast	towst
★6	bloe	blo	blow

Long O phoneme

Solve the clues to fill in the missing letters in the crosswords. In each crossword frame you will find two different spellings for the long **O** phoneme. Use the word bank to help you.

1. You wash with this and it makes bubbles
2. A flower that smells nice and has thorns

Crossword 1:
- 1. (down)
- 2. _ O S _

3. The wind does this
4. An animal which rhymes with coat

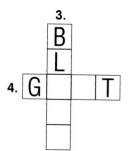

Crossword 3:
- 3. B L ...
- 4. G ... T

5. A round model of the world
6. The surface we drive on

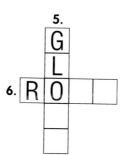

Crossword 5:
- 5. G L O ...
- 6. R O _ _

7. In water you can sink or _ _ _ _
8. You smell with it

Crossword 7:
- 7. F L T
- 8. N _ E

9. Footballers score in this
10. An antonym for fast

Crossword 9:
- 9. G
- 10. S L _ _

11. You can sail in this
12. You have ten of these on your feet

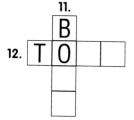

Crossword 11:
- 11. B
- 12. T O _ _

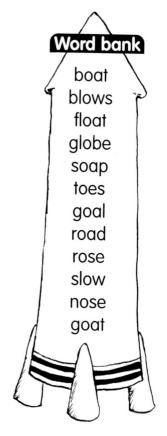

Word bank

boat
blows
float
globe
soap
toes
goal
road
rose
slow
nose
goat

Long U phoneme

The answers to these puzzles have the long **U** phoneme. This phoneme can be spelt four ways:
- **U** + silent **E** as in *cube* and *rule*
- **UE** as in *blue* and *due*
- **EW** as in *few* and *blew*
- **OO** as in *food.*

Circle the words with a long **U** phoneme and write them in the table.

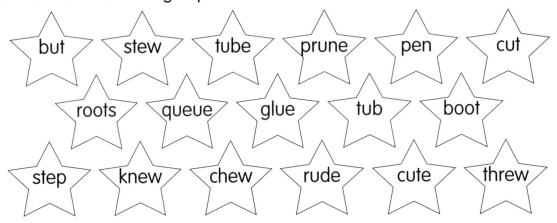

but · stew · tube · prune · pen · cut

roots · queue · glue · tub · boot

step · knew · chew · rude · cute · threw

U + silent E as in *rule*	UE as in *blue*	OO as in *food*	EW as in *blew*

Choose a phoneme or blend from each column to make words with the long **U** phoneme. You can use each phoneme or blend as many times as you like. Write the words you make in the rocket.

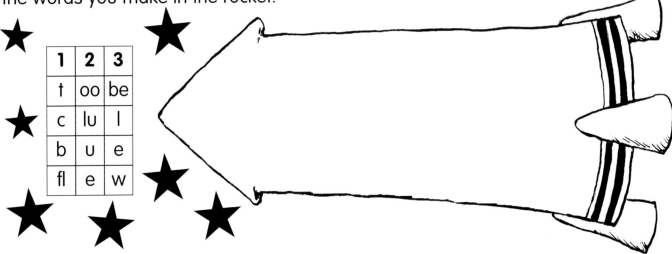

1	2	3
t	oo	be
c	lu	l
b	u	e
fl	e	w

Phonics and Spelling 3

Long U phoneme

Unjumble the words below and write them on the lines, then circle them in the wordsearch. All the words have the long **U** phoneme. The words can only be read across or down.

R	T	R	T	R	U	E
U	O	U	C	H	P	V
D	O	L	H	L	O	G
E	L	E	E	M	O	R
T	S	D	W	M	L	E
O	J	U	N	E	Y	W
O	S	C	H	O	O	L

1. Jenu _____

2. deru _____

3. rute _____

4. lopo _____

5. loscho _____

6. oto _____

7. sloot _____

8. leur _____

9. werg _____

10. wech _____

Circle the long **U** phoneme in these words, for example, resc(ue).

volume   igloo   argue   kangaroo   toothbrush   fortune

confuse   toothpaste   prune

Now circle the correct spelling for these words.

★1	croo	crew	crue
★2	glue	glew	gloo
★3	babewn	babone	baboon
★4	rewl	rule	ruel
★5	moon	mewn	mune
★6	chew	chue	choo

Various long vowel phonemes

The answers to these puzzles have long vowel phonemes. For example, *make* (long **A**), *tree* (long **E**), *time* (long **I**), *hole* (long **O**) and *cute* (long **U**). Circle the words that have long vowel phonemes. Write them in the table below in their vowel groups

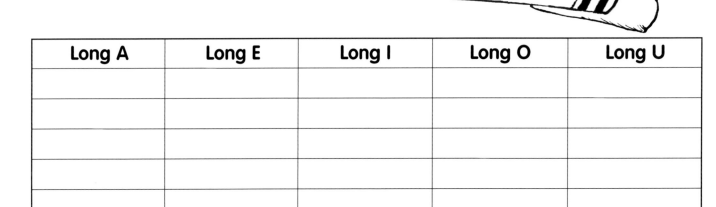

tail sight flies play slow blue use dew
toes home school week she mine pie race say
date sea beans here line goat go new

Long A	Long E	Long I	Long O	Long U

Choose one letter from each column in the grid to make a four-letter word with a long vowel phoneme. You can use the different letters as many times as you like, but you must use one from each column, for example, |c|a|k|e| = **cake**. Then draw a table like the one above and fill in your words. The pictures will give you clues to some of the words you could make.

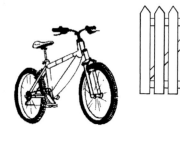

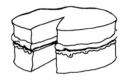

1	2	3	4
c	a	a	e
w	e	k	k
b	o	e	l
g	u	i	t

Various long vowel phonemes

Choose a tile from each column to make a four-letter word with a long vowel phoneme. Use the tiles as many times as you like but you must have one from each column to make the word. The pictures and clues will help you. Write the words you make in the table. One example has been completed for you.

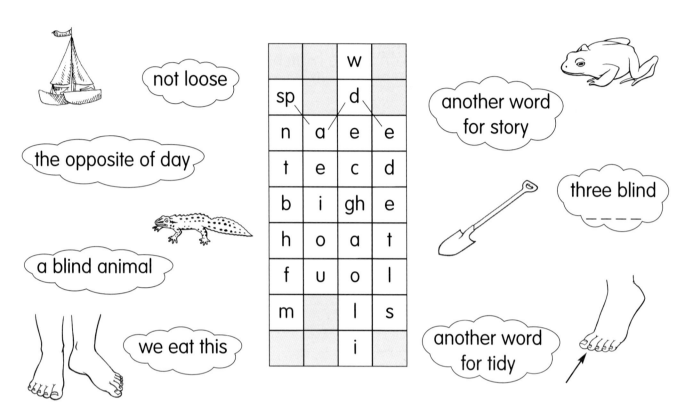

not loose	another word for story
the opposite of day	three blind
a blind animal	another word for tidy
we eat this	

Long A	Long E	Long I	Long O	Long U
spade				

★ ★ ★ ★ ★ ★ ★ ★ ★ ★

Final blends with D

Final blend means a blend at the end of a word. The words in these puzzles have final blends that end with **D**. The final blends could be **LD**, **ND** or **RD**, for example, *bold*, *land* and *hard*. Read the words below and join them to the matching pictures with a line.

hand

pond

card

bird

sword

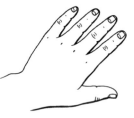

Join the words to the definitions or clues.

★1 The past tense of hold   end

★2 The finish, where something stops   held

★3 Unable to see   sand

★4 The place in a race after second   third

★5 You can build castles with this on the beach   blind

Final blends with D

All the words in this puzzle end with the final **D** blends **LD**, **ND** or **RD**. Write the missing words in the sentences. Circle any other words you can see with a final **D** blend.

Word bank			
wand	word	gold	cold
send	hard	held	wind

★ I am going to _____ birthday cards to my pen pal and my aunt.

★ In the storm the _____ blew very hard.

★ I _____ my baby sister's hand when we crossed the road.

★ The test was very _____ and I didn't get many answers right.

★ We were told to be quiet and not say a _____.

★ The water in the pond was so _____ it was turning into ice.

★ My gran gave me a _____ necklace for Christmas.

★ The fairy waved her magic _____.

Final blends with K

Final blend means a blend at the end of a word. The words in these puzzles all have final blends that end with **K**. The final blends could be **LK**, **NK**, **RK** or **SK**, for example, *milk*, *ink*, *work* and *mask*.

Read the words and join them to the matching picture with a line.

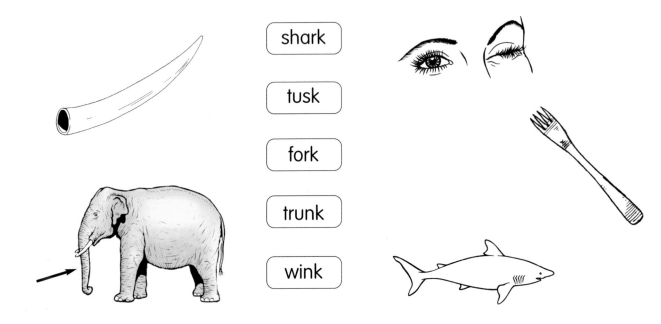

shark

tusk

fork

trunk

wink

These **compound** words have been muddled up. Join them together and write the complete words on the lines. Each word has a final **K** blend in it and one has been done for you.

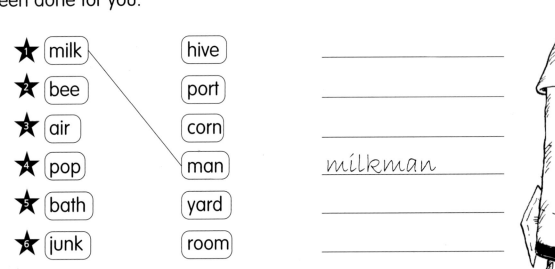

⭐1 milk   hive
⭐2 bee   port
⭐3 air   corn
⭐4 pop   man
⭐5 bath   yard
⭐6 junk   room

_____

_____

_____

milkman

_____

_____

Final blends with K

Find your way across the page. Join a planet to a star to make a word with a final **K** blend. Then match the word to the clue and write your answer in the rocket.

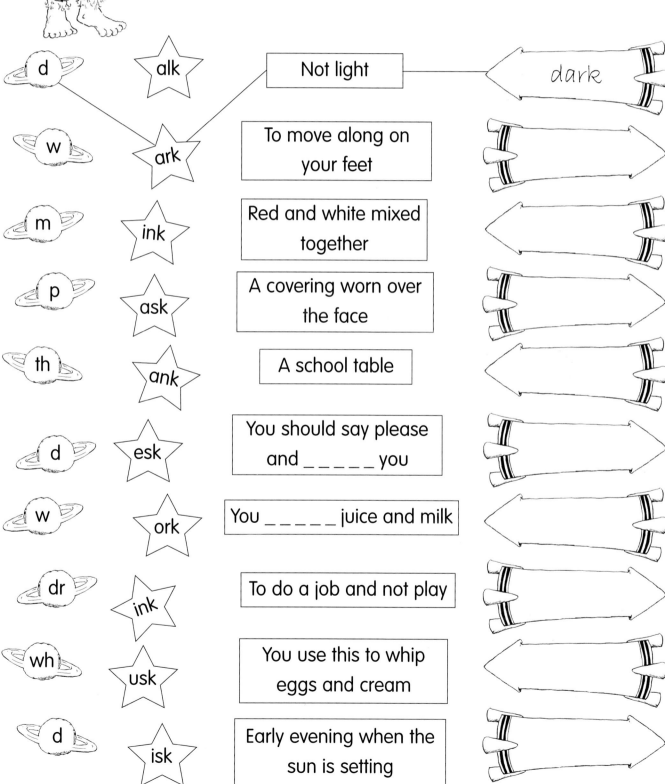

Planet	Star
d	alk
w	ark
m	ink
p	ask
th	ank
d	esk
w	ork
dr	ink
wh	usk
d	isk

Not light → dark

To move along on your feet

Red and white mixed together

A covering worn over the face

A school table

You should say please and _ _ _ _ _ _ you

You _ _ _ _ _ _ juice and milk

To do a job and not play

You use this to whip eggs and cream

Early evening when the sun is setting

Final blends with P

Final blend means a blend at the end of a word. The words in these puzzles all have final blends that end with **P**. The final blends could be **LP**, **MP**, **RP** or **SP**. For example, *he**lp**, ca**mp**, ha**rp*** and *cri**sp***.

Read the words and join them to the matching pictures with a line.

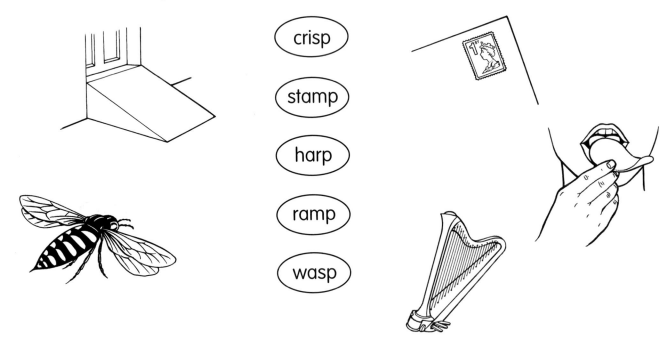

crisp

stamp

harp

ramp

wasp

Match the definitions in the rockets to the correct stars.

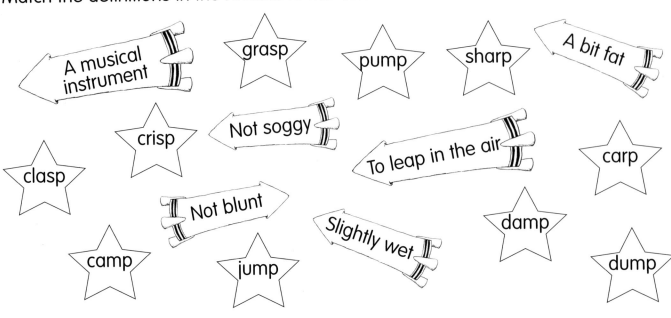

A musical instrument

grasp

pump

sharp

A bit fat

crisp

Not soggy

To leap in the air

carp

clasp

Not blunt

Slightly wet

damp

camp

jump

dump

Phonics and Spelling 3

Final blends with P

Use the letters in the planet to make words that end with **MP**. Start with a phoneme or blend from the outer ring, add a vowel from the middle ring and the final **MP** blend. Make as many words as you can. Write the words you make in the table in lower-case letters.

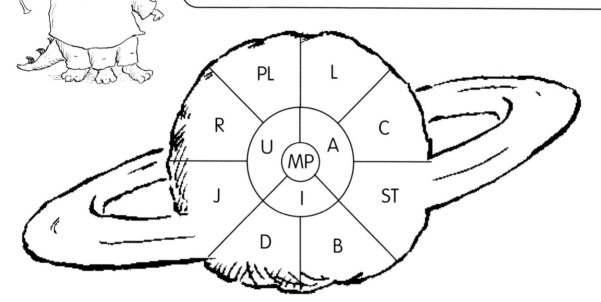

AMP words	IMP words	UMP words

Use some of the words from the table above to fill the gaps in these sentences.

★1 On our school __ __ __ __ we slept in tents and our sleeping bags got __ __ __ __ in the rain.

★2 On the cross-country run I had to __ __ __ __ over a tree __ __ __ __ __ __.

★3 If you __ __ __ __ your head you may get a bruise or a __ __ __ __ __.

Final blends with T

Final blend means a blend at the end of a word. The words in these puzzles all have final blends that end with **T**. The final blends could be **LT**, **NT**, **RT** or **ST**. For example, *felt*, *mint*, *dart* and *best*.

Read the words and join them to the matching pictures with a line.

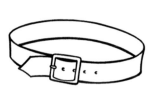

ant

tent

belt

nest

raft

Use the letters in the diamond to make words that end with **NT**. Start with a phoneme or blend from the outer diamond, add a vowel from the middle diamond and the final **NT** blend. Make as many words as you can. Write the words you make in the rocket.

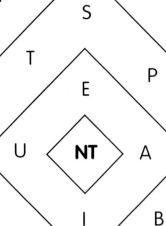

Final blends with T

Use the letters in the triangle to make words that end with **ST**. Use a phoneme from the first column, add a vowel from the middle and the final **ST** blend. Make as many words as you can. Write the words you make in the table in lower case letters.

AST words	EST words	IST words	OST words	UST words

Join the words in the rockets to the correct definition or clue.

1. art — An antonym for last

2. blunt — Another word for quick

3. fast — North, South, East and _____

4. first — Not sharp

5. West — Drawing and painting

Final blends with B, F, L, M and N

The words in this puzzle have final blends that end with **B, F, L, M** or **N**, for example, *bulb, shelf, girl, warm, brown*. Read the words in the rockets, find the picture that matches and join them with a line.

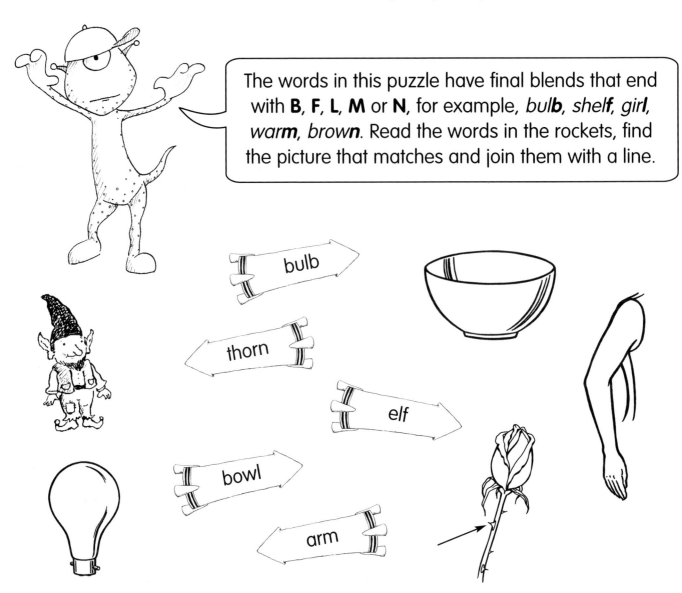

Unjumble the anagrams in the stars to make rhyming pairs of words. Write them in the stars then join each rhyming pair with a line. One has been unjumbled for you.

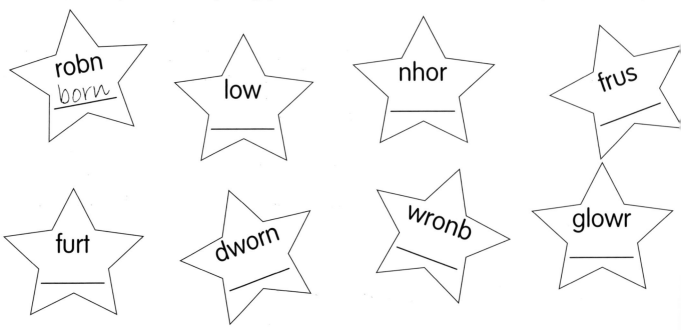

Final blends with **M** and **N**

Use the letters in the triangle to make words that end with **RN** or **WN**. Use a consonant from the first column, a vowel from the second, then **R** or **W** and the final **N**. Make as many words as you can. Write the words you make in the table.

ARN words	ERN words	ORN words	URN words	AWN words	OWN words
		born			

Use the letters in the triangle to make words that end with **RM** or **LM**. Use a consonant from the first column, a vowel from the second, then **R** or **L** and a final **M**. Make as many words as you can. Write the words you make in the table.

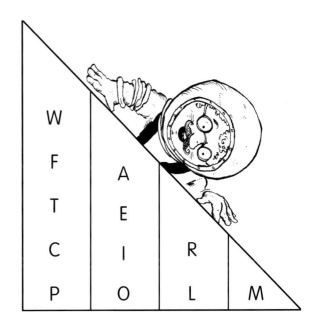

ARM words	ERM words	IRM words	ORM words	ALM words	ILM words

Words that end in FF, LL and SS

The words in this puzzle end in double **FF**, **LL**, or **SS**, for example, *off*, *hill* and *dress*. One-syllable words that end in **L** always have a double **L**, for example, *doll*. Solve the clues below and write the answers in the crossword in capital letters. At the end of each clue you will see how many letters are in the answer and what the last two letters are. Use the word bank to help you.

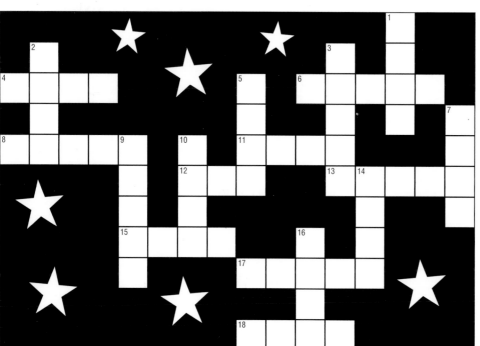

Word bank

WALL	TALL
WELL	PILL
BELL	DOLL
DRESS	FULL
HISS	PUFF
SHELL	GLASS
DRILL	CROSS
SNIFF	FUSS
OFF	PULL

ACROSS
4. Holds up the roof **LL** (4)   **6.** Use this to make holes **LL** (5)   **8.** Windows are made of this **SS** (5)   **11.** If you are very upset about something you may, make a _ _ _ _ _ **SS** (4)   **12.** An antonym for on **FF** (3)   **13.** Snails have one **LL** (5)   **15.** An antonym for empty **LL** (4)   **17.** A girl may wear one **SS** (5)   **18.** You may have to take one of these if you are ill **LL** (4)

DOWN
1. An antonym for push **LL** (4)   **2.** An antonym for short **LL** (4)   **3.** Another word for angry **SS** (5)   **5.** If you are out of breath you may _ _ _ _ and pant **FF** (4)   **7.** Ring this on your bike **LL** (4)   **9.** You may do this with your nose if you have a cold **FF** (5)   **10.** Toy for a little girl **LL** (4)   **14.** The noise of a snake **SS** (4)   **16.** You draw water from this **LL** (4)

Words that end in LE

These words all end in **LE** which sounds like **UL**, for example, *table*. When there are two consonants before the **LE** the vowel phoneme is short as in *scramble* and *bottle*. When there is only one consonant, the vowel phoneme is long as in *cradle* and *rifle*.

Write the letters in the boxes. All the words end with **LE**. Some words have picture clues and some have written clues.

1.

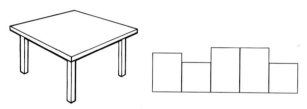

4.

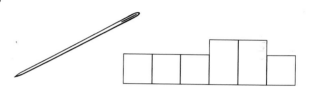

2. The centre

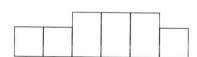

5. Your mother or father's brother

3.

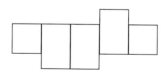

6. Pool of rain water

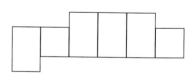

Each puzzle below contains five words ending in **LE**. Find and circle the words. One example is done for you.

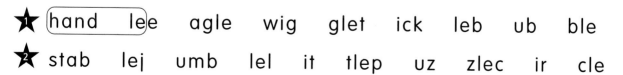

★ 1 hand   le e   agle   wig   glet   ick   leb   ub   ble

★ 2 stab   lej   umb   lel   it   tlep   uz   zlec   ir   cle

Verbs in the past tense with ED

Verbs are sometimes called doing words as they describe what people do, for example, *talk* and *laugh*. When we talk about the past, we use the **past tense**. Verbs in the past tense sometimes end with **ED**. For example, *Yesterday I talk**ed** and laugh**ed**.*

Add the missing words to this table.

Present tense	Past tense		Present tense	Past tense
play			talk	
	helped			worked
jump			row	
	growled			painted
lick			crash	
	pushed			washed

Read the clues and unjumble these past tense verbs with **ED**. Write the words on the lines.

1. The ice cream [detlem] in the sun. _____

2. After it [dewson] the ground was white. _____

3. I [pudemp] up the tyres on my bike. _____

4. I was feeling ill so I [dateys] in bed all day. _____

5. The ambulance [dusher] to the car crash. _____

6. I lost my necklace and we [dookel] everywhere for it. _____

7. I [dockle] the back door with a key. _____

8. I [dawesh] my mum's car and she gave me some money. _____

9. On Saturday I stayed up late and [dechatw] TV. _____

10. At the end of the race I [swolde] down because I was tired. _____

Verbs in the past tense with ED

Verbs are sometimes called doing words as they describe what people do, for example, *play* and *work*. When we talk about the past we use **past tense verbs**, for example, *Yesterday I played and worked*. The answers to these puzzles are all past tense verbs. Read the instructions for each section very carefully to find out how to change the verbs from present to past tense, then write the past tense verbs on the lines.

These verbs end in two or more consonants. To make them past tense verbs, just add **ED**, for example, *crash – crashed*.

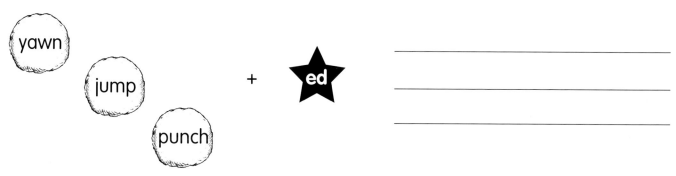

These verbs end in a vowel + **Y** or **W**. To make them past tense verbs, just add **ED**, for example, *spray – sprayed* and *show – showed*.

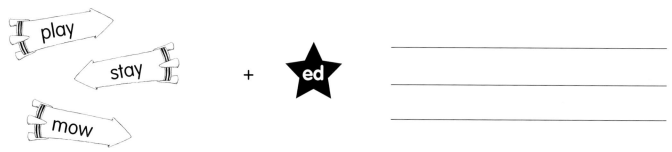

These verbs end in **E**. To make them past tense verbs, just add **D** because the **E** is already there, for example, *save – saved*.

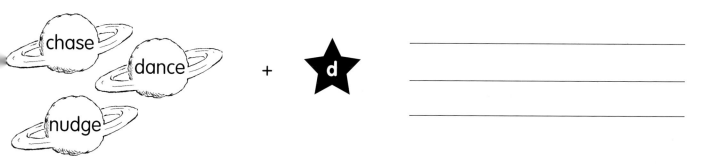

Verbs in the past tense with **ED**

These verbs have a short vowel phoneme and one final consonant. To turn them into past tense verbs you need to double the final consonant and add **ED**, for example, *shop – shopped*. Write the past tense verbs in the empty boxes.

★1	stop		p			
★2	pat		t			
★3	scrub		b			
★4	flap	+	p	+	ed	
★5	beg		g			
★6	plan		n			
★7	trip		p			

These verbs have a consonant before a final **Y**. To make them past tense verbs, change the **Y** to **I** and add **ED**, for example, *hurry – hurried*. Write the past tense verbs in the empty boxes.

★1	hurry	⟶	hurr					
★2	try	⟶	tr					
★3	carry	⟶	carr					
★4	cry	⟶	cr	+	i	+	ed	
★5	spy	⟶	sp					
★6	worry	⟶	worr					
	marry	⟶	marr					

Verbs with ING

Verbs are sometimes called doing words as they describe what people do, for example, *laugh* and *play*. We can add **ING** to verbs to describe an action that lasts and is not over quickly, for example, *Today the boy is laughing. Yesterday the boy was laughing. Tomorrow the boy will be laughing.*

Add the missing words to this table.

Past tense	Present tense	Verb with ING		Past tense	Present tense	Verb with ING
played	play			talked	talk	
helped		helping		worked		working
jumped	jump			rowed	row	
growled		growling		crashed	crash	
licked				cried	cry	
pushed	push			hurried	hurry	

Read the clues and unjumble these anagrams with **ING**. Write the words on the lines.

1. The ice cream was [tleginm] in the sun. _____

2. It is [winsgon] and the ground is turning white. _____

3. I was [gipunmp] up the tyres on my bike. _____

4. I am not well, so I am [gatnysi] in bed today. _____

5. The ambulance was [gushrin] to the car crash. _____

6. I have lost my necklace and we are [nooklig] everywhere for it.

_____

7. I was [gocklin] the back door with a key when it broke. _____

8. I was [gawhnis] my mum's car when I got my clothes wet. _____

9. On Saturdays I like staying up late and [inchtawg] TV. _____

10. It is the end of the race and I am [swonlig] down because I am tired.

_____

Verbs with ING

Verbs are sometimes called doing words as they describe what people do, for example, *laugh* and *play*. We can add **ING** to verbs, for example, *Today we are reading*. *Yesterday we were reading*. *Tomorrow we will be reading*. Read the instructions for each section very carefully to find out how to add **ING**, then write the words with **ING** on the lines.

If verbs end in two or more consonants, you can add **ING** without changing the spelling of the verb, for example, *crash – crashing*.

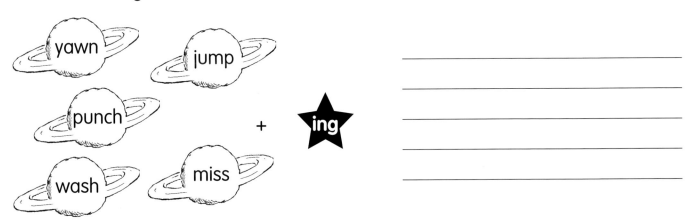

If verbs end in **Y** or **W**, you can add **ING** without changing the spelling of the verb, for example, *spray – spraying* and *show – showing*.

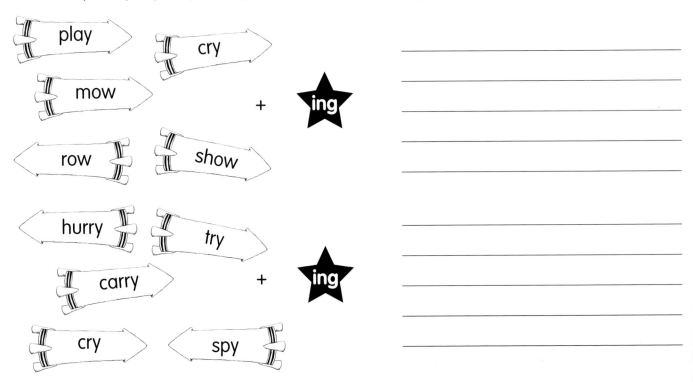

Verbs with ING

The verbs in the table below have short vowel phonemes and one consonant at the end. You need to double the final consonant and then add **ING**, for example, *shop – shopping*. Write the verbs with **ING** in the empty boxes.

★1	stop		p		
★2	pat		t		
★3	scrub	+	b	+ ing	
★4	flap		p		
★5	beg		g		

The verbs in the table below end in **E**. You need to take off the **E** then add **ING**, for example, *save – saving*. Write the verbs with **ING** in the empty boxes.

★1	chase	→	chas		
★2	dance	→	danc		
★3	nudge	→	nudg	+ ing	
★4	wiggle	→	wiggl		
★5	like	→	lik		

Verbs with ED and ING

Verbs are sometimes called doing words as they describe what people do. **ED** and **ING** can be added to verbs, for example, *jump – jumped/jumping*. Look at the picture clue and unjumble the anagram (which is a verb). Write the verbs on the lines. Then write them again with **ED** and **ING**. The example shows you what to do.

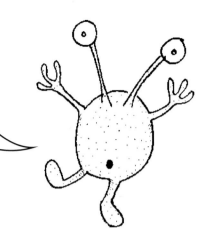

		Word	With ED	With ING
Example:	ujmp	jump	jumped	jumping
1.	oph	_____	_____	_____
2.	erac	_____	_____	_____
3.	ryc	_____	_____	_____
4.	veaw	_____	_____	_____
5.	pary	_____	_____	_____
6.	swon	_____	_____	_____
7.	ickk	_____	_____	_____
8.	pots	_____	_____	_____
9.	brucs	_____	_____	_____
10.	hups	_____	_____	_____

Verbs with ED and ING

Add the missing words to the table and write a sentence for the verbs that are in the shaded boxes on the lines below.

	Verb	Verb + ED	Verb + ING
★1	play		
★2		cried	
★3			showing
★4	bake		
★5		watched	

★1	
★2	
★3	
★4	
★5	

The words in this table are irregular verbs that do not follow the rules and do not end in **ED** in the past tense. You will need to learn and practise these verbs. Write a sentence for each verb in the shaded boxes on a separate piece of paper.

Present tense	Past tense	Verb with ING		Present tense	Past tense	Verb with ING
see	saw	seeing		sit	sat	sitting
go	went	going		come	came	coming
think	thought	thinking		fly	flew	flying
run	ran	running		write	wrote	writing
blow	blew	blowing		take	took	taking
catch	caught	catching		grow	grew	growing
make	made	making		buy	bought	buying
fight	fought	fighting		teach	taught	teaching
freeze	froze	freezing		lose	lost	losing
bite	bit	biting		shine	shone	shining

Words with similar patterns and meanings

Sometimes long words have smaller words inside them. When this happens they can have similar meanings. These words are often compound words, which are made when small words are joined together to make longer words, for example, *bedroom* and *bathroom*.

The answers to the clues all start with the word **HAND**. Work out what they are and write them in the crossword in capital letters.

Word bank

HANDLE
HANDFUL
HANDKERCHIEF
HANDBAG
HANDCUFFS

ACROSS

1. A small amount   **3.** A policeman puts these on a thief's wrists   **4.** You use this to blow your nose

DOWN

1. A lady puts her purse and keys in this   **2.** You pull this to open a drawer

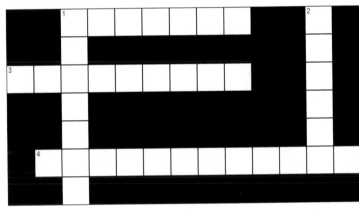

These words all contain the word **BALL**. Look at the clues to work out what they are and write them in the crossword in capital letters.

Word bank

NETBALL   BALLOON
FOOTBALL   BASKETBALL

ACROSS

3. Bounce the ball and shoot into a hoop   **4.** Two teams kick a ball

DOWN

1. A playground sport
2. Blow this colourful object up for a party

Words with similar patterns and meanings

The answers in these puzzles all contain the word **FOOT**, but they don't all begin with **FOOT**. Look at the clues to work out what they are. The number tells you how many letters there are in the word. Circle the answers in the wordsearch.

1. A round shape to kick about (8)
2. A mark in the sand made by a foot (9)
3. If you are not wearing shoes or socks you are going _____ (8)
4. If you walk very quietly, no one will hear your _____ (9)

H	B	W	F	R	T	B	P	H
Y	Y	F	O	M	T	A	Z	D
R	N	W	O	J	L	R	L	H
F	O	O	T	S	T	E	P	S
P	T	T	B	K	K	F	L	M
Q	M	Z	A	H	L	O	N	Q
N	F	J	L	C	D	O	V	T
L	M	T	L	Y	X	T	X	N
F	O	O	T	P	R	I	N	T

Circle the word in the star that goes with all of the words in the rocket to make a compound word. Write these words underneath.

1.
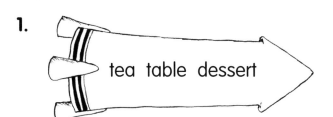 tea table dessert

 pot spoon cloth

_____

2.
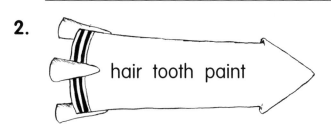 hair tooth paint

 paste brush drier

_____

3.
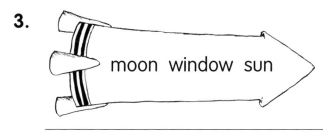 moon window sun

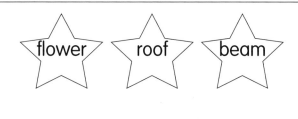 flower roof beam

_____

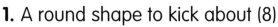

Words with similar patterns and meanings

The words in this puzzle start with the word **HEAD**. Read the clues and join the words in the rockets to the word in the planet to make your answers. Write them on the lines next to the clues.

lights

head

mistress

ache

lines

phones

master

Clues

1. A pain in the head _____

2. They help drivers see in the dark _____

3. A man in charge of a school _____

4. A woman in charge of a school _____

5. Use them to listen to music _____

6. The titles of stories in a newspaper _____

Read the clues. Unjumble the anagrams to make words with **DAY** and write them on the lines.

★1 This **DAY** comes before today. STEERYYAD _____

★2 This **DAY** is the day we are in. YADOT _____

★3 This **DAY** is the opposite of night-time. TIEDYAM _____

★4 This **DAY** comes before Tuesday. DOMYAN _____

★5 This **DAY** happens when the sun rises. BAKEYARD _____

★6 This **DAY** helps us to see. TAGDHIYL _____

★7 This **DAY** means to be miles away in your head. MADERADY _____

Phonics and Spelling 3

The prefixes UN and DIS

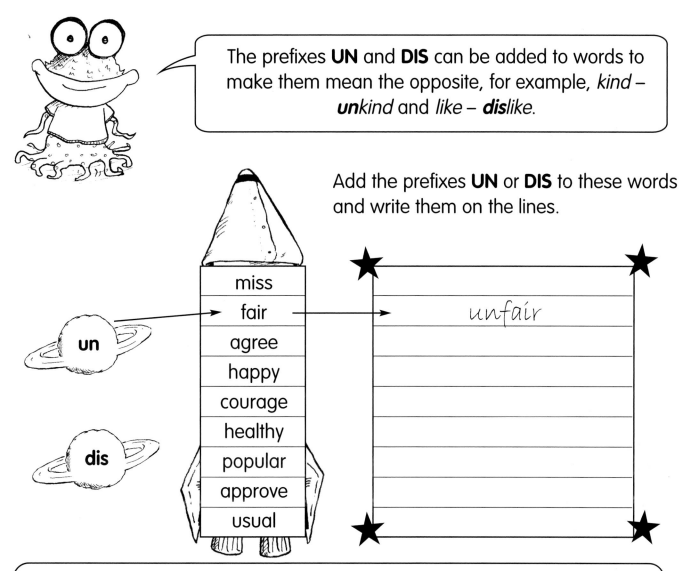

The prefixes **UN** and **DIS** can be added to words to make them mean the opposite, for example, *kind* – **un***kind* and *like* – **dis***like*.

Add the prefixes **UN** or **DIS** to these words and write them on the lines.

un

dis

miss
fair
agree
happy
courage
healthy
popular
approve
usual

unfair

Read the clues and unjumble these words with **UN** and **DIS** and write your answers on the lines. Look first to see if they have **UN** or **DIS** in them.

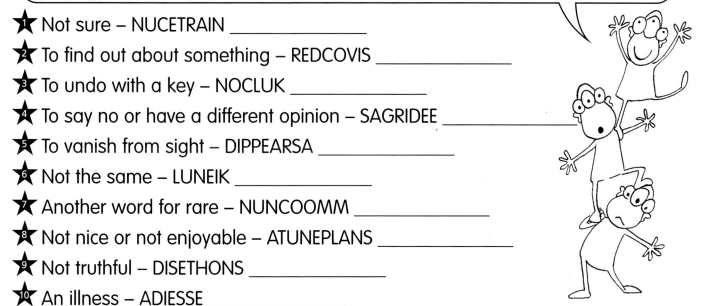

★1 Not sure – NUCETRAIN _____

★2 To find out about something – REDCOVIS _____

★3 To undo with a key – NOCLUK _____

★4 To say no or have a different opinion – SAGRIDEE _____

★5 To vanish from sight – DIPPEARSA _____

★6 Not the same – LUNEIK _____

★7 Another word for rare – NUNCOOMM _____

★8 Not nice or not enjoyable – ATUNEPLANS _____

★9 Not truthful – DISETHONS _____

★10 An illness – ADIESSE _____

The prefixes DE, RE and PRE

These words begin with the prefixes **DE**, **RE** and **PRE**. **DE** often means 'away' or 'get smaller' as in *de*part and *de*crease. **RE** often means 'again' or 'back' as in *re*peat and *re*verse. **PRE** often means 'before' as in *pre*historic and *pre*pare.

Join the words to the correct prefix and write them in a rocket. One has been done for you.

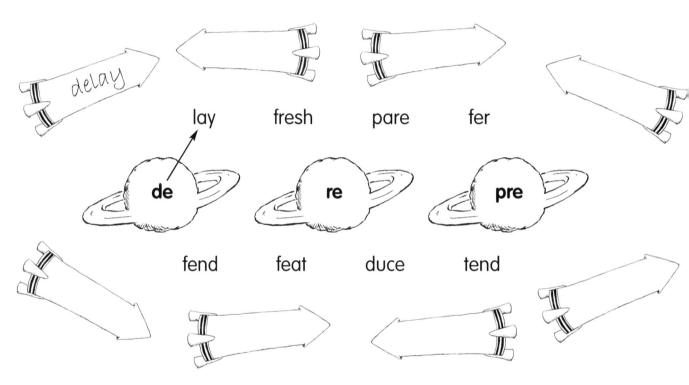

delay

lay   fresh   pare   fer

de   re   pre

fend   feat   duce   tend

Sort these **DE**, **RE** and **PRE** words into alphabetical order and write them on the lines. You will need to look at the letter that follows each prefix.

★1	defy	~~decay~~	detective	depart	demand
	decay				
★2	replace	research	reward	recycle	reverse
★3	prevent	pretend	prefix	prepare	precaution

Phonics and Spelling 3 © Folens (copiable page)

Words that describe ways of speaking

The verbs on this page can be used instead of the verb *say*, *said* or *saying*. They describe how someone is speaking in more interesting ways.

Put the missing phonemes in these verbs to complete the sentences. The phonemes that you need are in the stars. You can use each phoneme as many times as you like.

1. My teacher (__ s k __ __ __) me a tricky question.

2. I (__ __ __ __ __ per __ __) to my sister, so that no one else could hear me.

3. The policeman was (__ __ ou __ in __), so that the crowd could hear him.

4. I put my hand up to (__ __ sw __ __) the questions.

5. My aunty (sc __ __ __ __ __ ed), 'Get that mouse out of here!'

6. I (ca __ __ __ __ d) out to my friend across the street.

7. 'What a funny joke,' the man (l __ __ __ gh __ __ __).

8. My brother and I were (__ __ gui __ g) over who was the biggest.

Stars: i, l, g, h, e, t, u, ea, sh, au, s, r, m, d, a, wh

Animals can't speak (except in cartoons) but they can communicate with each other. What noises do they make? Read the words, look at the pictures and join them together correctly. Then write a sentence for each animal using these words.

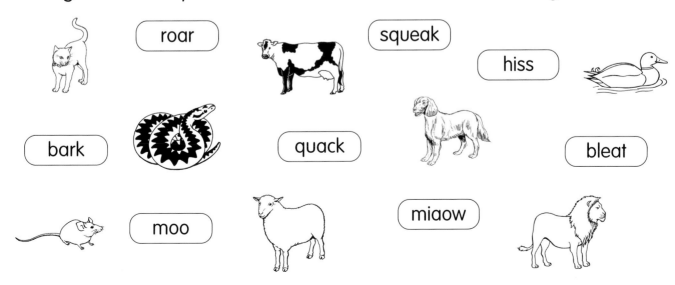

roar   squeak   hiss

bark   quack   bleat

moo   miaow

Synonyms

Synonyms are words that mean the same or nearly the same as another word, for example, *small – little*. Read the sentences. Circle the word below that is a synonym for the underlined word.

Example: The monster was <u>big</u>.   ugly   (large)   old

★1 The baby couldn't <u>talk</u>.	speak	walk	stand
★2 I like my <u>house</u> and garden.	horse	home	room
★3 The soup was in the <u>bowl</u>.	dish	plate	boat
★4 My mum was very <u>cross</u>.	hot	angry	sad
★5 I am going to <u>shut</u> the door.	shout	close	open
★6 The animals were <u>noisy</u>.	nasty	hungry	loud
★7 Tick the <u>correct</u> answer.	right	wrong	closed
★8 Fish swim in the <u>sea</u>.	sand	tank	ocean
★9 I am <u>tired</u>.	tall	sleepy	unhappy
★10 The test was <u>easy</u>.	long	hard	simple

Join the words that mean the same or nearly the same.

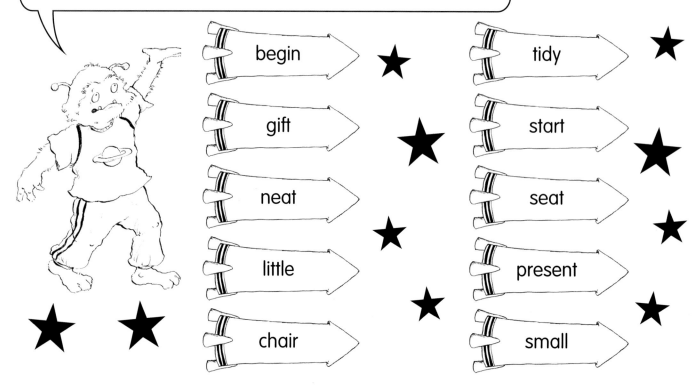

begin   ★   tidy   ★

gift   ★   start   ★

neat   ★   seat   ★

little   ★   present

chair   small   ★

★ ★

Synonyms

These words are synonyms (words that mean the same or nearly the same as another word), but the letters in each word are muddled up. Look at the picture clues and write the two synonyms on the lines beside the pictures.

1.  _sad_   ~~das~~ phunpay

2.  _____ kics lil

3.  _____ den fishin

4.  _____ tabo hips

5.  _____ gab sace

6.  _____ gur tam

7.  _____ gub scinet

     Phonics and Spelling 3

Words with TCH

The letter string **TCH** is found in words such as *ditch* and *fetch*. **TCH** should not be confused with the phoneme **CH**. Sort the words in the planets, stars and rockets into rhyming groups in the table below.

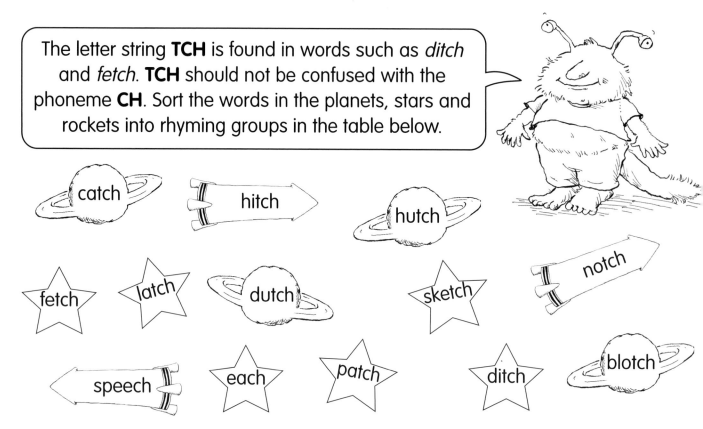

Words that rhyme with...					
atch	**itch**	**etch**	**otch**	**utch**	**teach**

Choose a phoneme or blend, then a vowel to make words that end in **TCH**. Write your words on the lines next to the clues.

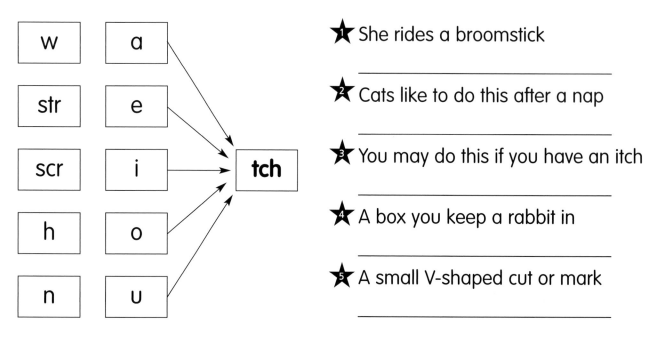

w   a

str   e

scr   i   tch

h   o

n   u

⭐**1** She rides a broomstick

_____

⭐**2** Cats like to do this after a nap

_____

⭐**3** You may do this if you have an itch

_____

⭐**4** A box you keep a rabbit in

_____

⭐**5** A small V-shaped cut or mark

_____

Words with TCH

Choose a final letter string for these words and write them on the lines next to the clues.

| pea |
| pi |
| wa |
| pa |
| scree |

ch

or

tch

★1 This is a fruit

★2 A rugby field is also called a rugby _ _ _ _ _

★3 Wear it on your wrist to tell the time

★4 Sew one of these over a hole in your trousers

★5 Another word for scream

_____

_____

_____

_____

_____

Circle the **TCH** letter string in these words, for example, cat(ch)ing.

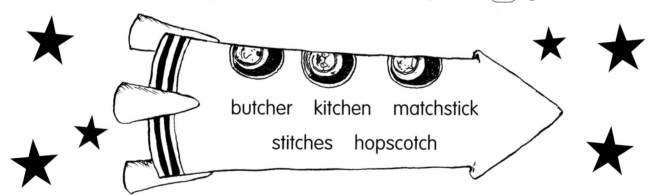

butcher   kitchen   matchstick
stitches   hopscotch

Find the words in the rocket above in this wordsearch and circle them.

Q	B	U	T	C	H	E	R	J	E	U	O
M	N	Y	K	I	T	C	H	E	N	H	B
W	S	T	I	T	C	H	E	S	F	G	S
L	M	A	T	C	H	S	T	I	C	K	Z
H	O	P	S	C	O	T	C	H	R	D	K

Words with DGE

The words in these puzzles end in **DGE**, for example, *ridge* and *dodge*. Join the phoneme or blend to the **DGE** letter strings below and write in the box. An example has been done for you.

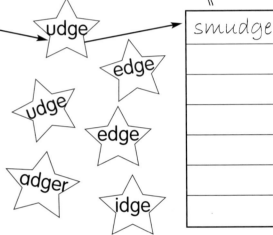

Example	A dirty mark	sm
★ 1	Slide down snowy hills on this	sl
★ 2	A soft and sugary sweet	f
★ 3	Cross this to get over a river	br
★ 4	You can keep food cold in this	fr
★ 5	A row of bushes	h
★ 6	A black and white animal	b

smudge

In these lists of **DGE** words there is one made-up word. Cross out the word that isn't real.

1. edge ledge badge bridge dedge

2. dodge bidge ridge nudge fudge

3. wedge lodge hedge widge sledge

Eight of the real words in the rocket are in the wordsearch below. Find and circle them.

  ★ ★

Q	W	G	H	E	D	G	E	T	D	Y	P	F
S	H	R	J	D	K	L	P	C	O	V	N	U
B	R	I	D	G	E	U	B	A	D	G	E	D
X	Z	D	B	E	N	G	S	Y	G	V	N	G
E	I	G	D	V	T	R	S	L	E	D	G	E
W	Q	E	M	N	X	Z	R	T	U	A	E	O

Words with DGE

I am an alien postman with lots of phonemes in my sack. They are parts of five **DGE** words but they have got muddled up. Sort them out and fill in the answers. You can use the phonemes as many times as you like.

⭐ A sheriff wears a silver one __ __ dge

⭐ A narrow shelf __ __ dge

⭐ If you're on a cliff, stay away from the __ dge

⭐ This person decides who wins a competition __ __ dge

⭐ To push someone with your elbow to make them notice something __ __ dge

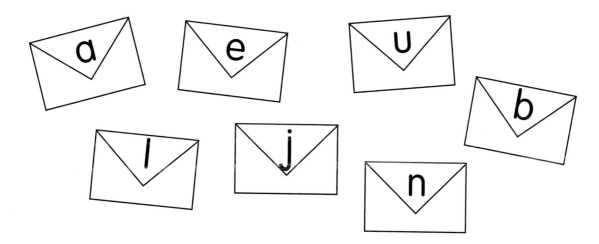

Look at the **DGE** words in the rockets. Join each word to another word that rhymes with it. Can you add more rhyming words?

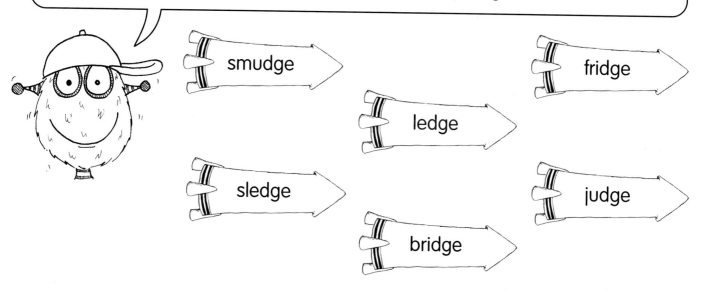

smudge

ledge

fridge

sledge

bridge

judge

Phonics and Spelling 3

Words that begin with K

K can have a hard C phoneme, or it can be a silent letter. When K is silent, it is always followed by N as in *knit*. When it has a hard C phoneme, it is followed by I or E as in *kick* and *key*. Exceptions to this rule are found in words that come from other countries, when K is followed by other letters as in *kangaroo*, *karate* and *koala*.

Using the phonemes in the stars, make as many words as you can that begin with K. Write them in the table. You can reuse the phonemes.

K with a hard C		Silent K	
kiln		knead	

Stars: o, k, i, ck, kn, f, ee, t, a, n, l, b, er, e, d, ea

Look at the phonemes and blends in the bricks and rearrange them to make eight words that begin with K.

⭐1 | gar | kan | oo | _____

⭐2 | ho | key | le | _____

⭐3 | ss | ki | _____

⭐4 | ck | ki | _____

⭐5 | ak | kay | _____

⭐6 | ll | ki | _____

⭐7 | lo | ki | am | gr | _____

⭐8 | la | ko | a | _____

Phonics and Spelling 3

Words that begin with K

Read the clues and write your answers on the spaceships. There are secret words in the shaded area that you will find when the walls are complete. Write the secret words in the rockets.

The answers to this puzzle all have **K** with a hard **C** phoneme.

1. Used to unlock a door
2. A colourful diamond you can fly
3. Boils water for tea
4. A room where food is cooked
5. A dog's house
6. He sits on a throne

Secret word

The answers to this puzzle all have **K** as a silent letter.

1. Where your legs bend
2. He wears armour and has a sword
3. To get down on your knees
4. The past tense of know
5. Use it to cut up your dinner
6. People do this to make jumpers
7. Tie this in your shoelace

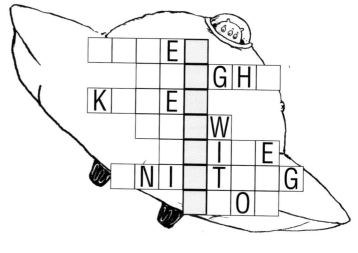

Secret words

 Sort the words you have made into alphabetical order. You will need to look at the second, third and fourth letters.

Adding Y

Y can be added to lots of words to make adjectives. Adjectives are describing words, for example, *bumpy* and *spotty*. These are the rules for adding **Y**:

- Two final consonants ➜ add **Y** as in *bu**mp** – bu**mp**y*.
- Word ends in a long vowel and one consonant ➜ add **Y** as in *sp**ook** – sp**ook**y*.
- Word ends in a short vowel and one consonant ➜ double the last letter and add **Y** as in *bag – baggy*.
- Word ends in a final **E** ➜ take off the **E** and add **Y** as in *scar**e** – scar**y***.

Make the words in the stars into adjectives and write each one in the sentence in which it fits best.

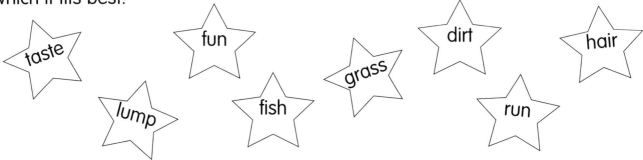

taste   fun   dirt   hair   lump   fish   grass   run

1. I had to clean my shoes because they were _____.

2. The pizza was very _____ and I ate it all.

3. The _____ clown made us laugh.

4. The porridge was cold and _____.

5. The jelly hadn't set and it was still _____.

6. The monster was big and _____.

7. The garden is _____ and green.

8. My cat's dinner smells _____.

Circle the five **Y** words hidden in this letter puzzle and write them on the line.

s t r i   p y l   u c   k y s   a n d   y r   u s   t y s   m e l   l y

_____

Adding Y

The phonemes in the rocket spell five weather adjectives that end in **Y**. Write them in the boxes. You can use a phoneme as many times as you like.

1.

2.

3.

4.

5.

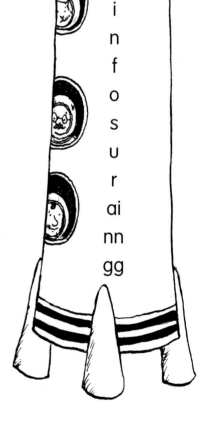

Below are rhyming pairs of words that end in **Y** but one is an anagram. Unjumble the anagram and write the word on the line.

1. sunny – yunfn _____

2. gusty – study _____

3. chilly – ilyls _____

4. batty – taycht _____

5. foggy – gybog _____

6. spicy – yic _____

Phonics and Spelling 3

Plural nouns

We use singular nouns when there is one item and plural nouns for more than one, for example, *one **bed**, two **beds***. To make most plurals we just add **S**, but it isn't always so simple. There are some rules for making plurals. Read each rule carefully, then look at the pictures and clues for each puzzle. The pictures show singular nouns which you must make into plurals. Write the plural nouns in the stepword puzzles in capital letters.

Rule Add **S** to words that do not end in **S**, **O**, **CH**, **SH**, **X** and **Z**, for example, *bag – bags*.

1.

2. You read these

3. You enter rooms through these

4. Find these on envelopes

5.

5.
| T |
4. S | | | |
| E |
3.
D | | E
2. B | |
1. C H | | |

Rule Add **ES** to words that do end in **S**, **O**, **CH**, **SH**, **X** and **Z**, for example, *fox – foxes*.

1.

2. Tissues come in these

3. These can be made into chips

4. Like bowls

5.

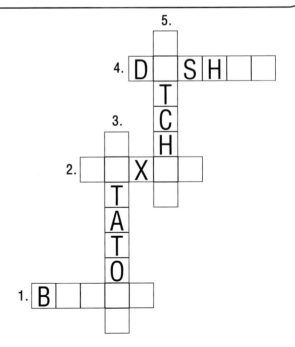

5.
4. D | S H |
T
C
H
3.
2. | X |
T
A
T
O
1. B | | |

Plural nouns

We use singular nouns when there is one item and plural nouns for more than one, for example, *one bed, two beds*. To make most plurals we just add **S**, but it isn't always so simple. There are some rules for making plurals. Read each rule carefully, then look at the pictures and clues for each puzzle. The pictures show singular nouns which you must make into plurals. Write the plural nouns in the stepword puzzles in capital letters.

Rule When nouns end **F** or **FE**, change the **F** to **V** and add **S** or **ES,** for example, *elf – elves* and *half – halves*.

1. Worn around your neck

2.

3. A synonym for robbers

4.

5. They eat little pigs

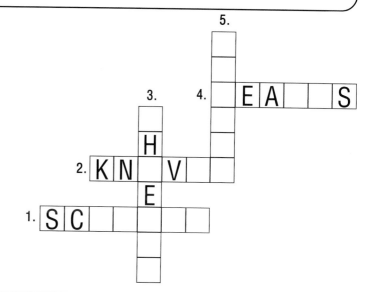

Rule When nouns end in a consonant + **Y**, change the **Y** to **I** and add **ES**, for example, *story – stories*. When nouns end in a vowel + **Y** just add **S**, for example, *boy – boys*.

1. Baby dogs

2. Things you play with

3.

4. There are seven of these in a week

5. When we are born, we are _____

Irregular plural nouns

 We use singular nouns when there is one item and plural nouns for more than one. There are rules for creating regular plurals, but the plurals in this puzzle are irregular. Find the plural forms for these nouns. The word bank will help you. Write the plural form next to the noun. The number tells you how many letters there are in each plural. Then circle the plurals in the wordsearch. The words can only be read across and down.

1. man (3) _____   **2.** woman (5) _____   **3.** child (8)

_____   **4.** foot (4) _____   **5.** tooth (5) _____

6. person (6) _____   **7.** goose (5) _____   **8.** mouse (4)

_____   **9.** sheep (5) _____   **10.** door (5) _____

11. skirt (6) _____   **12.** fish (4) _____   **13.** reindeer (8)

_____   **14.** pan (4) _____   **15.** glass (7) _____

S	C	I	D	O	O	R	S	D	L	X
G	E	E	S	E	J	E	T	B	R	C
K	P	P	N	X	T	I	M	I	C	E
F	E	E	T	K	E	N	T	X	P	C
S	M	O	Y	L	E	D	C	F	B	S
H	E	P	M	B	T	E	Q	I	W	K
E	N	L	C	N	H	E	N	S	O	I
E	P	E	T	T	F	R	M	H	M	R
P	F	P	A	N	S	S	Q	K	E	T
R	M	C	H	I	L	D	R	E	N	S
V	L	Z	N	G	L	A	S	S	E	S

Word bank

GLASSES
REINDEER
PANS
MEN
CHILDREN
TEETH
GEESE
SHEEP
DOORS
WOMEN
FEET
PEOPLE
MICE
FISH
SKIRTS

Plural nouns revision

We use singular nouns when there is one item and plural nouns for more than one, for example, *one apple, two apples*. Look at the clues. Use the rules for making plural nouns to spell the words correctly in the crossword. Be careful as five answers are irregular plural nouns. The word bank will help you.

Word bank

MEN	BOYS	CUPS	MICE	PENS	FOXES	HANDS	SHEEP	TRAYS
WIVES	CALVES	HALVES	HORSES	LADIES	SHELLS	BRUSHES		
FEET	BUBBLES	WATCHES	CHERRIES	CHURCHES	TEETH			

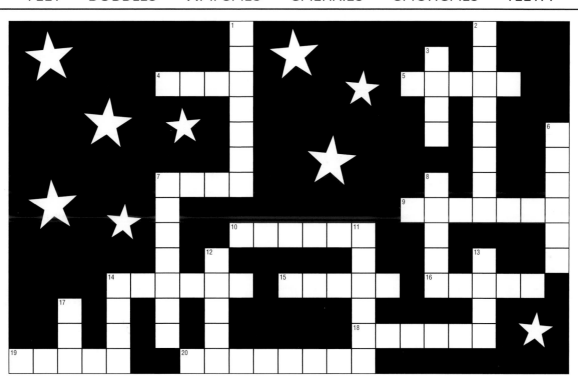

ACROSS

4. We walk on these (4)　**5.** Husbands are married to these (5)　**7.** An antonym for girls (4)　**9.** We use these to paint (7)　**10.** Sandwiches can be cut into these (6)　**14.** Baby cows (6)　**15.** These animals chase rabbits (5)　**16.** We get wool from them (5)　**18.** Another word for women (6)　**19.** At the end of our arms (5)　**20.** Christians go there on Sundays (8)

DOWN

1. We use these to tell the time (7)　**2.** Small round red fruits (8)　**3.** Three blind _ _ _ _(4)　**6.** We can ride these animals (6)　**7.** You find these in the bath (7)　**8.** We use these to carry things (5)　**11.** You find these on the beach (6)　**12.** We brush them twice a day (5)　**13.** We use these to write (4)　**14.** We drink from these (4)　**17.** An antonym for women (4)

Silent letters

Silent letters are letters in words that you cannot hear. Look at the examples below:

- Silent **K** – **k**nee
- Silent **G** – **g**nome
- Silent **W** – **w**riggle
- Silent **B** – lam**b**
- Silent **N** – autum**n**
- Silent **C** – s**c**ience
- Silent **H** – w**h**isk

Circle the silent letters in these words.

kneel   gnat   wrong

wreck   wheel   whisper

knit

Write the silent letters in these words. The letters you need are in the planets.

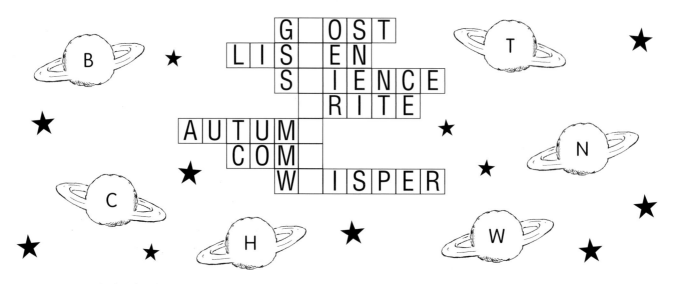

G O S T
L I S S E N
S I E N C E
R I T E
A U T U M
C O M
W I S P E R

Silent letters

Read the clues and look at the pictures. All the answers have silent letters. Write your answers in the stepword puzzles. Some silent letters are written in to help you.

1. As people grow older they get these on their faces

2.

3. The season before winter

4. A dog will do this to a bone

5.

6. These are baby sheep

7.

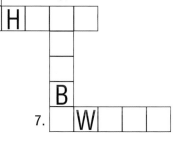

1. The colour of snow

2.

3.

4.

5. A type of paper used to cover presents
6. An antonym for ask
7. To move like a worm does

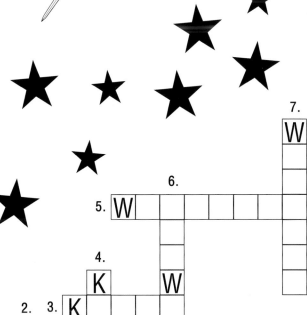

Compound words

Compound words are formed when small words are joined together to make longer words, for example, *sunflower* and *grasshopper*. Look at the pictures. Join together a small word from each column to make a longer compound word. Write your answers by the pictures. One has been done for you.

space	mill	★ 1	_____
tooth	roads	★ 2	_____
cross	brush	★ 3	_____
table	ship	★ 4	*tablecloth*
wind	cloth	★ 5	_____
rain	room	★ 6	_____
jelly	bow	★ 7	_____
bed	fish	★ 8	_____
thunder	paper	★ 9	_____
news	storm	★ 10	_____

Compound words

Find the compound word that best completes each sentence and write it in the space.

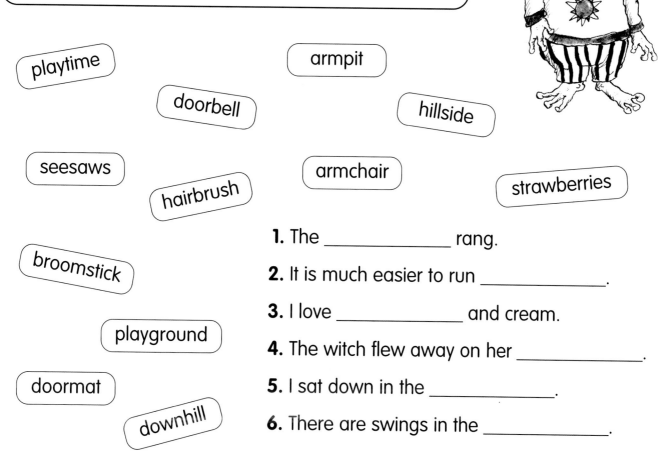

playtime

armpit

doorbell

hillside

seesaws

armchair

hairbrush

strawberries

broomstick

playground

doormat

downhill

1. The _____ rang.

2. It is much easier to run _____.

3. I love _____ and cream.

4. The witch flew away on her _____.

5. I sat down in the _____.

6. There are swings in the _____.

Join the compound words in the rockets to their synonyms (words that mean the same).

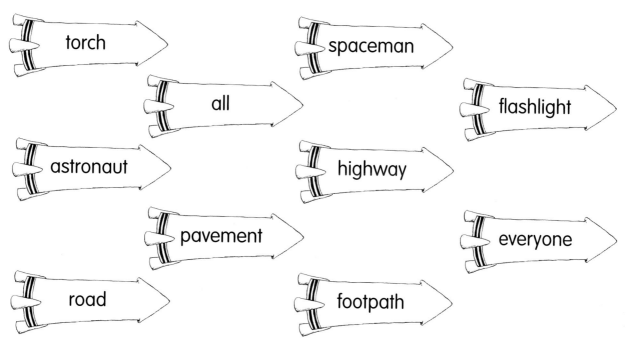

torch

spaceman

all

flashlight

astronaut

highway

pavement

everyone

road

footpath

The suffix LY

LY can be added to adjectives to make words which tell us more about verbs, for example, *The dog barked loudly*. In this sentence *barked* is the verb and *loudly* tells us how the dog barked.

Add **LY** to these adjectives to complete the sentences like the example.

Example: The **slow** snake moved **slowly**.

1. The **quiet** cat purred _____.
2. The **neat** children wrote _____.
3. The **nervous** driver drove _____.
4. The **shy** girl smiled _____.
5. The **quick** runner ran _____.
6. The **kind** nurse treated people _____.
7. The **nice** lady spoke _____.
8. The **bold** puppy barked _____.
9. The **loud** teenager yelled _____.
10. The **sweet** bird sang _____.

These adjectives end in **Y** so before you add **LY** you must change the **Y** to **I**, for example, *crazy – crazily*. Add **LY** to these words and write them on the lines.

| happy |
| funny |
| noisy | Change the **Y** to **I** → + **LY**
| lazy |
| pretty |

_____

_____

_____

_____

_____

Adjectives

Adjectives are words that tell us more about nouns. They tell us what kind, what size or what colour, for example, *an **old** house, a **small** house, a **white** house*. Find the missing adjectives in the clues below and write them in the crossword.

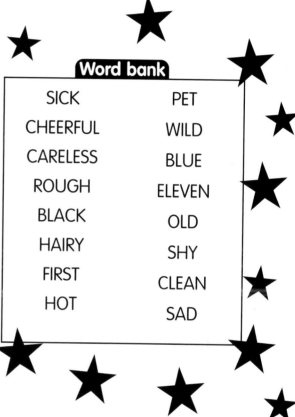

Word bank

SICK	PET
CHEERFUL	WILD
CARELESS	BLUE
ROUGH	ELEVEN
BLACK	OLD
HAIRY	SHY
FIRST	CLEAN
HOT	SAD

ACROSS

3. The _____ boy cried when he broke his toy. (3)   **5.** The _____ children broke the window. (8)   **7.** I don't like bananas when they are _____. (5)   **9.** The _____ boy was always smiling. (8)   **11.** Some dogs are very _____. (5)   **13.** I love my _____ dog.   **14.** The _____ girl would not speak in assembly. (3)   **15.** The _____ soup soon warmed me up. (3)

DOWN

1. Lions, tigers and elephants are _____ animals. (4)   **2.** The _____ sky didn't have any clouds. (4)   **3.** My _____ friend stayed home from school. (4)   **4.** I showed my _____ hands to my mum after I washed them. (5)   **6.** The football team of _____ boys won the cup. (6)   **8.** The _____ house was nearly falling down. (3)   **10.** The _____ man in the race won a gold medal. (5)   **12.** The boat sank in the _____ sea. (5)

The suffixes ER and EST

Adjectives are words that tell us more about nouns. The suffixes **ER** and **EST** can be added to most adjectives. **ER** is used to compare nouns and **EST** tells us which is the most as in *the **bigger** dog, the **biggest** dog*.

The rules for adding **ER** and **EST**:
- Final **E** → add **R** or **EST** as in *nice – nicer, nicest*.
- Final consonants or a long vowel phoneme add **ER** or **EST** as in *cold – colder, coldest*.
- Final **Y** after a consonant → change **Y** to **I** and add **ER** or **EST** as in *funny – funnier, funniest*.
- Final consonant with a short vowel phoneme → double the consonant and add **ER** or **EST** as in *hot – hotter, hottest*.

Add **ER** and **EST** to the adjectives in these sentences by following the rules above.

1. **small** – A cat is _____ than a horse and a mouse is the _____ of the three.

2. **happy** – The boy who came second was _____ than the boy who came last, but the winner was the _____.

3. **brave** – I think a cat is _____ than a mouse but a lion is the _____.

4. **old** – My mum is _____ than me and my grandma is the _____.

5. **silly** – My twin sister is _____ than me, but my little brother is the _____.

6. **neat** – My desk is _____ than my friend's, but she says hers is the _____.

Join each adjective to its antonym (opposite). One has been completed for you.

faster	longest
shortest	thinner
wider	slower
easier	youngest
oldest	prettiest
ugliest	richer
poorer	harder

The suffixes ER and EST

Choose a phoneme from each column to make adjectives that end in **ER** and **EST**. The first one has been done for you.

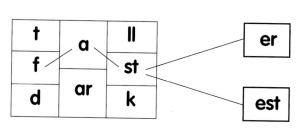
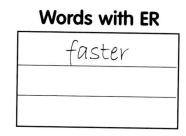

Words with ER

faster

Words with EST

fastest

These adjectives have long vowel phonemes so you can just add **ER** and **EST** to them.

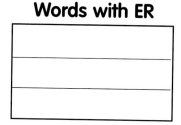
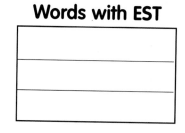

Words with ER

Words with EST

These adjectives end in **E** so just add **R** and **ST** to them.

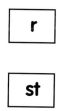
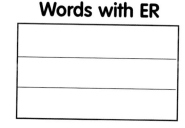

Words with ER

Words with EST

These adjectives have short vowel phonemes and one final consonant which must be doubled before you add **ER** and **EST** to them.

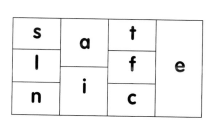

Words with ER

Words with EST

These adjectives end in **Y** that must be changed to **I** before you add **ER** and **EST** to them.

h	u	pp	~~y~~ change to i
b	a	gg	
f	a	nn	

er

est

Words with ER

Words with EST

The suffixes FUL and LESS

The suffixes **FUL** and **LESS** can make words have opposite meanings, for example, *care**ful** – care**less***. Remember that **FUL** ends in one **L** and **LESS** ends in **SS**. Some words can have one suffix, but not the other, for example, *awful* is a word but *awless* is not, *endless* is a word but *endful* is not.

Unjumble the anagrams in the planets to make words that end in **FUL**. The clues in the boxes will help you. Write your words in the empty rockets.

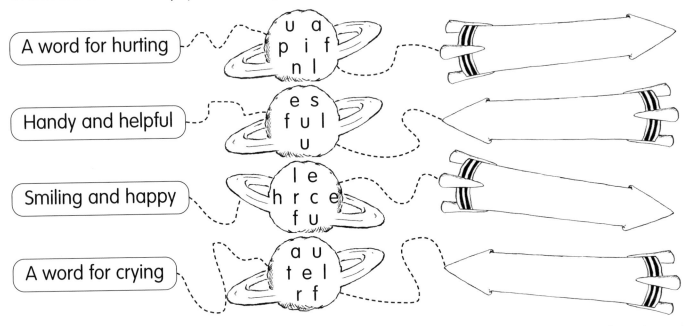

A word for hurting

Handy and helpful

Smiling and happy

A word for crying

Unjumble these anagrams in the stars to make words that end in **LESS**. The clues in the boxes will help you. Write your words in the empty rockets.

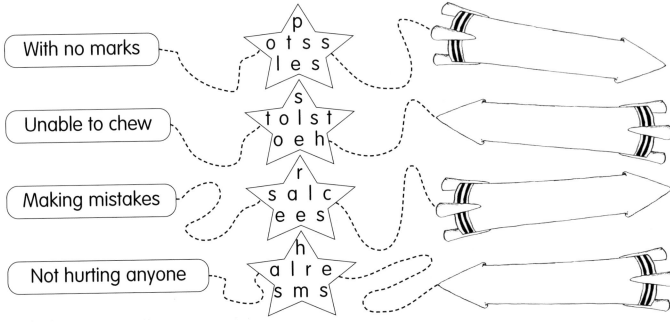

With no marks

Unable to chew

Making mistakes

Not hurting anyone

Phonics and Spelling 3

© Folens (copiable page)

Contractions

Contractions of words are formed when words are shortened. An apostrophe takes the place of the missing letter or letters and two words become one word, for example, *are not* becomes *aren't*. The apostrophe takes the place of the missing **O**. Unusual contracted words are *will not* which becomes *won't* and *shall not* which becomes *shan't*.

Join the long form of these words to their contracted forms.

Words with NOT

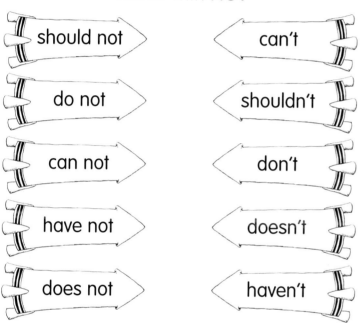

should not

do not

can not

have not

does not

can't

shouldn't

don't

doesn't

haven't

Words with WILL

we will

I will

she will

they will

he will

I'll

she'll

we'll

he'll

they'll

Words with AM and ARE

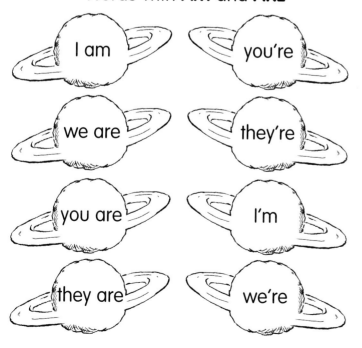

I am

we are

you are

they are

you're

they're

I'm

we're

Put the apostrophe in the correct place in these words.

1. d o n t
2. y o u r e
3. w e r e
4. h a v e n t
5. d o e s n t
6. t h e y r e
7. s h e l l
8. c a n t

Antonyms

Start at the top step and fill in the antonyms (opposites) for the numbered words written down. The first word of each puzzle has been written in for you.

B **H** I **M**

1. HER 2. WOMAN
3. DAY 4. HERE
5. START
6. DIDN'T
7. SHALLOW
8. WORK

1. SMALL
2. STOP
3. UNDER
4. LEFT   5. FAT
6. YES   7. ON
8. SLOW   9. FROM

To find the antonyms for these words, unjumble these anagrams and then write your answers on the lines.

1. **up** – wond _____

2. **odd** – neev _____

3. **dry** – tew _____

4. **sad** – pypha _____

5. **in** – tuo _____

6. **pretty** – lugy _____

7. **worst** – steb _____

8. **empty** – lulf _____

9. **young** – dol _____

10. **first** – stal _____

Now find four pairs of antonyms of your own and write them below.

1. _____   3. _____

2. _____   4. _____

Phonics and Spelling 3 © Folens (copiable page)

Alphabetical order

In a dictionary, words are listed in alphabetical order from **A** to **Z**. When words begin with the same letter, the second letter is used to sort them, for example, *bag*, *bed* and *bread*. Put these words into alphabetical order by looking at their second letters and write them on the lines.

⭐1 another   away   at

_____

⭐2 cry   car   children

_____

⭐3 did   dad   door

_____

⭐4 left   look   last

_____

⭐5 now   name   next

_____

⭐6 pig   past   play

_____

Sort the words in the planets into alphabetical order on the word wall to find the hidden message in the shaded bricks.

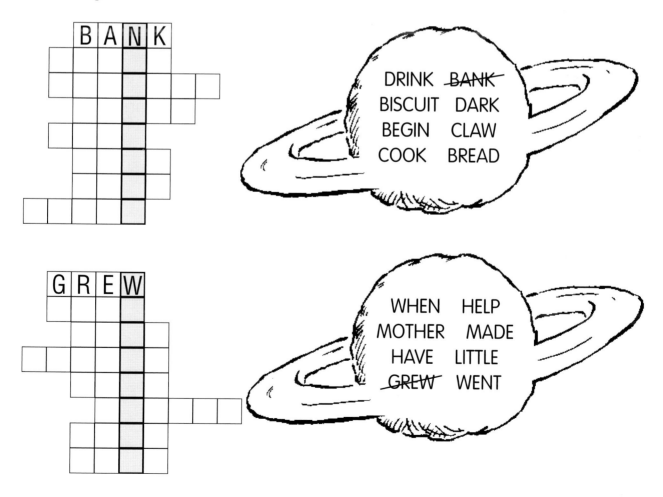

BANK

DRINK ~~BANK~~
BISCUIT DARK
BEGIN CLAW
COOK BREAD

GREW

WHEN   HELP
MOTHER   MADE
HAVE   LITTLE
~~GREW~~   WENT

Phonics and Spelling 3

The prefixes NON, CO, ANTI and EX

The following prefixes can be added to the start of words. They usually have these meanings and they are sometimes followed by a hyphen.

- **NON** means 'not' as in *non-fiction*.
- **CO** means 'together' or 'with' as in *co-operate*.
- **ANTI** means 'against' as in *antifreeze*.
- **EX** means 'out of' or 'from' as in *exit*.

Look at the three words in each section and choose the best one for each sentence. Write them on the lines.

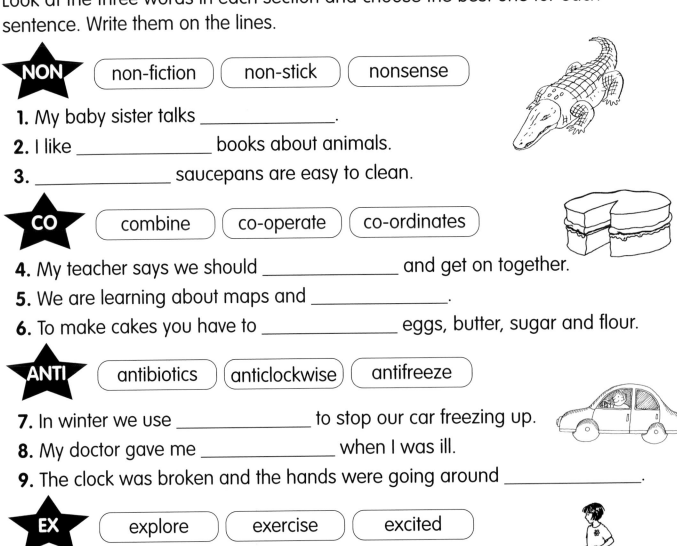

NON ⭐ (non-fiction) (non-stick) (nonsense)

1. My baby sister talks _____.

2. I like _____ books about animals.

3. _____ saucepans are easy to clean.

CO ⭐ (combine) (co-operate) (co-ordinates)

4. My teacher says we should _____ and get on together.

5. We are learning about maps and _____.

6. To make cakes you have to _____ eggs, butter, sugar and flour.

ANTI ⭐ (antibiotics) (anticlockwise) (antifreeze)

7. In winter we use _____ to stop our car freezing up.

8. My doctor gave me _____ when I was ill.

9. The clock was broken and the hands were going around _____.

EX ⭐ (explore) (exercise) (excited)

10. My friend and I wanted to _____ the caves.

11. I am _____ about my birthday party next week.

12. Healthy food and _____ will make you fit.

Homonyms

Homonyms are words that are spelt the same way but have more than one meaning, for example, *The weather is **cold**. I have a bad **cold**. I lit the **fire**. I can **fire** a gun.* Each of these homonyms has two meanings. Read the pairs of sentences and choose a homophone that best fits each pair.

1. He jumps over the _____ at the beach.

   He _____ goodbye to his dad.

2. My _____ helps me tell the time.

   I like to _____ cartoons on TV.

3. I threw a _____ for my dog to chase.

   I use glue to _____ things.

4. I washed the dishes in the _____.

   The old boat began to _____.

Read the clues and write the homonyms in the wordwall.

★1 Not heavy
★2 This goes in a letterbox or mailbox
★3 A game between two teams or people
★4 The part of a car where you can put luggage
★5 These are on your fingers and toes
★6 An antonym for work
★7 Not yours
★8 The season after winter

Homophones

A homophone is a word that is pronounced the same as another word, but with a different spelling and meaning, for example, *wood – would* and *tied – tide*.

What is the homophone? Read the clues and write a homophone for the underlined word in the crossword in capital letters.

ACROSS
1. <u>Where</u> are the missing pens?   **3.** We threw the <u>waste</u> into the bin.   **4.** I was pleased when I <u>won</u> the race.   **6.** There are seven days in a <u>week</u>.   **7.** I found a good <u>site</u> on the internet about sharks.   **8.** My job was to <u>pour</u> the cups of tea.
9. My mum's friend has a new baby <u>son</u>.

DOWN
2. In assembly we usually sit in <u>rows</u>.   **3.** We had to <u>wait</u> for a long time.
5. Walking up <u>stairs</u> is very tiring.   **6.** My friend asked if I <u>would</u> like to come too.
7. The farmer had to <u>sow</u> the seeds on the ground.   **8.** The cake was <u>plain</u> and boring.

Answers

■ PAGE 6

1. bananas	6. oranges
2. doughnuts	7. potatoes
3. grapefruit	8. raisins
4. ice cream	9. tomatoes
5. lemons	10. watermelon

kitten   lamb   mouse   newt   octopus   pig

■ PAGE 7

1.	rafte	after
2.	lalb	ball
3.	dulco	could
4.	rodo	door
5.	tea	eat
6.	fodo	food
7.	werg	grew
8.	eshou	house
9.	toni	into
10.	pumj	jump
11.	petk	kept
12.	tillet	little
13.	keam	make
14.	texn	next
15.	revo	over
16.	shup	push
17.	uckiq	quick
18.	nira	rain
19.	tessir	sister
20.	neth	then
21.	redun	under
22.	yvre	very
23.	henw	when
24.	r-axy	x-ray
25.	welloy	yellow
26.	ozo	zoo

1. apple	6. prince
2. door	7. rabbit
3. fish	8. umbrella
4. igloo	9. whale
5. lamp	10. zip

■ PAGE 8

1. after	6. brother
2. very	7. Tuesday
3. Saturday	8. December
4. before	9. tonight
5. morning	10. kitten

1. flow + er	6. to + day
2. Fri + day	7. be + gin
3. sis + ter	8. Ju + ly
4. yell + ow	9. twen + ty
5. nine + teen	10. go + ing

■ PAGE 9

One syllable	Two syllables
them	water
school	Monday
could	very
time	brother
boy	over

At school I learn how to read and spell.
I learn how to draw and count too.

■ PAGE 10

■ PAGE 11

■ PAGE 12

1. tap	6. cat
2. bag	7. had
3. flag	8. glad
4. sad	9. ran
5. bad	10. hat

1st syllable	2nd syllable	Complete word
st	atch	match
f	ad	glad
m	at	fat
gl	ack	black
bl	amp	stamp
cl	and	hand
l	an	plan
h	ab	grab
pl	amp	clamp
gr	amb	lamb

1. **a**nimal
2. pl**a**net
3. r**a**gdoll
4. milkm**a**n
5. teab**a**g
6. kneec**a**p
7. f**a**tter
8. cl**a**pping
9. c**a**pital
10. tr**a**pdoor

■ PAGE 13

1. bed
2. ten
3. West
4. hen
5. nest
6. peg
7. bell
8. sell
9. net
10. men

1st syllable	2nd syllable	Complete word
f	ed	red
dr	ep	step
st	est	test
t	ess	dress
r	ence	fence
b	ept	kept
n	em	them
k	edge	hedge
th	ext	next
h	est	best

1. blackb**e**rry
2. address
3. y**e**llow
4. b**e**droom
5. k**e**ttle
6. princ**e**ss
7. b**e**tter
8. ch**e**rry
9. p**e**tal
10. **e**xit

■ PAGE 14

1. pig
2. big
3. sick
4. hill
5. fins
6. zip
7. hiss
8. quick
9. king
10. this

1. picnic
2. pyram**i**d
3. w**i**nner
4. **i**nsect
5. g**i**ving
6. someth**i**ng
7. w**i**nter
8. mus**i**c
9. dustb**i**n
10. dolph**i**n

1st syllable	2nd syllable	Complete word
tw	in	thin
sw	id	kid
th	ink	drink
dr	im	swim
k	ig	twig
sw	im	prim
pr	iff	sniff
sn	itch	switch
spr	ip	skip
sk	ing	spring

■ PAGE 15

1. dog
2. hop
3. hot
4. mop
5. soft
6. sock
7. rock
8. pop
9. frog
10. pond

1. unl**o**ck
2. b**o**ttom
3. pr**o**per
4. hedgeh**o**g
5. forg**o**t
6. r**o**tten
7. **o**blong
8. ping-p**o**ng
9. t**o**ffee
10. l**o**llipop

1st syllable	2nd syllable	Complete word
st	ost	cost
c	oss	cross
cr	ock	lock
l	ob	job
j	op	stop
b	op	top
t	ob	rob
cl	oss	boss
str	ong	strong
r	ock	clock

■ PAGE 16

1. butterc**u**p
2. gr**u**mpy
3. b**u**ckle
4. unl**u**cky
5. b**u**cket
6. hicc**u**p
7. p**u**ppies
8. b**u**bble
9. d**u**mmy
10. chipm**u**nk

1. drum
2. bug
3. stuck
4. plug
5. mum
6. bus
7. mug
8. plus
9. brush
10. junk

1st syllable	2nd syllable	Complete word
tr	ut	shut
sh	ub	club
cl	ump	jump
h	unt	hunt
j	unk	trunk
t	uch	such
s	usk	tusk
gl	ust	crust
h	um	glum
cr	utch	hutch

Phonics and Spelling 3

■ PAGE 17

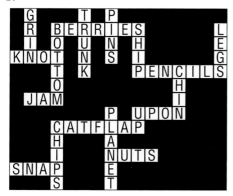

■ PAGE 18

```
P L A T E  G A M E S  S  L
H  R O B E  K Z N Z P  D
C A G E  L  T U N E  F  C
H G  T I M E  M K P  D  O
L Q  M  G R M N D F E  N
R P  I  A R L I C U  N  C
O D  N  R L L C B N  E  R
P E  E  L C N E B N  E  E
E K  B O N E  D E E E  T
X  K I T E  W A V E  D  E
B  T H R O N E  Y Q G  L
```

■ PAGE 19

(fight)	first	sit
(night)	list	bright
(bite)	(sight)	(white)
fist	fit	milk

1 li**gh**tning
2. exc**ite**d
3. mid**nigh**t
4. moonli**gh**t
5. pol**ite**

1. tight
2. tonight
3. knight
4. midnight
5. right

■ PAGE 20

A + silent E	AI	AY
snake	train	play
hate	sail	day
make	wait	spray

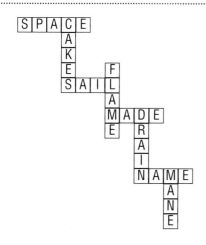

■ PAGE 21

```
a c e
d a y s
s n a i l
```
```
a p e
s t a y
n a i l s
```
```
M a y
c a s e
t r a i n
```
```
h a y
r a i n
s n a k e
```

■ PAGE 22

EE	EA	E
queen	each	he
green	clear	we
keep	meat	be

tea**cher** wee**kend** six**teen** be**fore** sun**beam** **ea**ting
teabag

1. cheese 2. dream 3. screen
4. speed 5. stampede 6. mean

■ PAGE 23

```
G R E E N
S H E
C L E A N
```
```
S L E E P
P E A S
T H R E E
```
```
F E E T
Y E A R
L E A F
```
```
S H E E P
B E A K
S T E A L
```

■ PAGE 24

I + silent E	Y	IE	IGH
pine	cry	flies	fight
wide	spy	tries	bright
write	sky	cries	night

bed**time** ins**ide** beeh**ive** to**nigh**t surpr**ise**
mid**nigh**t pol**ite** pantom**ime**

1	fite	(fight)	fiet
2	(bite)	bight	biet
3	spise	(spies)	spys
4	(fire)	fyre	fier
5	(mice)	myce	miec
6	(dry)	drie	drigh

■ PAGE 25

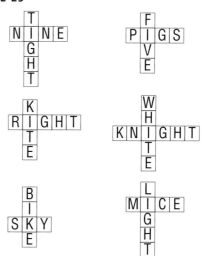

■ PAGE 26

O + silent E	OA	OE	O	OW
joke	loaf	goes	go	know
home	coal	toes	no	show

h**o**se Oct**o**ber wind**ow** yell**ow** vide**o** shad**ow**
expl**ode** elb**ow** tipt**oe**

1	bote	(boat)	bowt
2	(note)	noat	nowt
3	windoe	windo	(window)
4	pianoe	(piano)	pianow
5	toest	(toast)	towst
6	bloe	blo	(blow)

■ PAGE 27

```
  S
R O S E
  A
  P
```
```
  B
  L
G O A T
  W
  S
```
```
  G
  L
R O A D
  B
  E
```
```
  F
  L
N O S E
  A
  T
```
```
  G
  O
  A
S L O W
```
```
      B
      O
T O E S
      A
      T
```

■ PAGE 28

U + silent E as in *rule*	UE as in *blue*	OO as in *food*	EW as in *blew*
rude	glue	boot	threw
prune	queue	roots	chew
tube			stew
cube			knew

tool cool tube cube blue
clue flew flue cue

■ PAGE 29

```
R T R T R U E
U O U C H P V
D O L H L O G
E L E E M O R
T S D W M L E
T       M   W
O   J U N E Y
O   S C H O O L
```

vol**ume** igl**oo** arg**ue** kangar**oo** t**oo**thbrush
fort**une** conf**use** t**oo**thpaste pr**une**

1	croo	(crew)	crue
2	(glue)	glew	gloo
3	babewn	babone	(baboon)
4	rewl	(rule)	ruel
5	(moon)	mewn	mune
6	(chew)	chue	choo

■ PAGE 30

Long A	Long E	Long I	Long O	Long U
race	week	mine	home	use
tail	beans	sight	goat	school
say	here	pie	go	blue
date	she	flies	slow	new
play	sea	line	toes	dew

Long A	Long E	Long O	Long U
cake	beak	boat	cute
bake	week	coat	
wake	beat	goal	
gate	weak	goat	
wait	geek		
bait			
wail			

■ PAGE 31

A	E	I	O	U
spade	speed	spice	toad	boot
face	need	nice	boat	toot
tale	neat	night	hole	hoot
tail	bead	tight	fold	tool
fail	beat	fight	mole	fool
nail	feet	mice	foal	newt
hail	heat	might	node	fuel
male	meat	bide	tows	food
mail	feat	tide	mow	mood
made	teat	hide	bowl	mule
space				

■ PAGE 32

hand

pond

card

bird

sword

---

1. held
2. end
3. blind
4. third
5. sand

■ PAGE 33

1. I am going to **send** birthday cards to my pen pal and my aunt.
2. In the storm the **wind** blew very hard.
3. I **held** my baby sister's hand when we crossed the road.
4. The test was very **hard** and I didn't get many answers right.
5. We were told to be quiet and not say a **word**.
6. The water in the pond was so **cold** it was turning into ice.

7. My gran gave me a **gold** necklace for Christmas.
8. The fairy waved her magic **wand.**

■ **PAGE 34**

shark

tusk

fork

trunk

wink

1. beehive
2. airport
3. popcorn
4. milkman
5. junkyard
6. bathroom

■ **PAGE 35**

1. dark	6. thank
2. walk	7. drink
3. pink	8. work
4. mask	9. whisk
5. desk	10. dusk

■ **PAGE 36**

crisp

stamp

harp

ramp

wasp

Not soggy – crisp
To leap in the air – jump
Not blunt – sharp
Slightly wet – damp
A musical instrument – harp
A bit fat – plump

■ **PAGE 37**

AMP words	IMP words	UMP words
lamp	limp	lump
camp		stump
ramp		bump
damp		dump
stamp		jump
		rump
		plump

1. On our school **camp** we slept in tents and our sleeping bags got **damp** in the rain.
2. On the cross-country run I had to **jump** over a tree **stump.**
3. If you **bump** your head you may get a bruise or a **lump.**

■ **PAGE 38**

ant

tent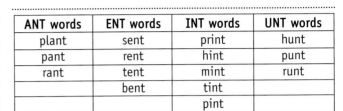

belt

nest

raft

ANT words	ENT words	INT words	UNT words
plant	sent	print	hunt
pant	rent	hint	punt
rant	tent	mint	runt
	bent	tint	
		pint	

■ **PAGE 39**

AST words	EST words	IST words	OST words	UST words
last	best	mist	lost	gust
mast	vest	fist	most	dust
vast	pest	list	post	must
past	rest			bust
fast				rust
				lust

1. art – Drawing and painting
2. blunt – Not sharp
3. fast – Another word for quick
4. first – An antonym for last
5. West – North, South, East and ____

■ **PAGE 40**

bulb

thorn

elf

bowl

arm

born – horn   owl – growl
surf – turf   brown – drown

■ **PAGE 41**

ARN words	ERN words	ORN words	URN words	AWN words	OWN words
barn	fern	corn	turn	lawn	down
tarn	tern	torn	burn	dawn	town
darn		born		fawn	

ARM words	ERM words	IRM words	ORM words	ALM words	ILM words
warm	term	firm	worm	palm	film
farm	perm		form	calm	

■ PAGE 42

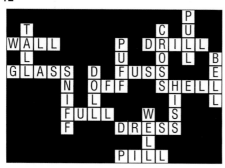

■ PAGE 43

1. table   3. apple   5. uncle
2. middle   4. needle   6. puddle

1. handle   eagle   wiggle   tickle   bubble
2. stable   jumble   little   puzzle   circle

■ PAGE 44

Present tense	Past tense	Present tense	Past tense
play	played	talk	talked
help	helped	work	worked
jump	jumped	row	rowed
growl	growled	paint	painted
lick	licked	crash	crash
push	pushed	wash	washed

1. The ice cream **melted** in the sun.
2. After it **snowed** the ground was white.
3. I **pumped** up the tyres on my bike.
4. I was feeling ill so I **stayed** in bed all day.
5. The ambulance **rushed** to the car crash.
6. I lost my necklace and we **looked** everywhere for it.
7. I **locked** the back door with a key.
8. I **washed** my mum's car and she gave me some money.
9. On Saturday I stayed up late and **watched** TV.
10. At the end of the race I **slowed** down because I was tired.

■ PAGE 45

yawned   played   chased
jumped   stayed   danced
punched   mowed   nudged

■ PAGE 46

1. stopped   5. begged   1. hurried   5. spied
2. patted   6. planned   2. tried   6. worried
3. scrubbed   7. tripped   3. carried   7. married
4. flapped   4. cried

■ PAGE 47

Past tense	Present tense	Verbs with ING
played	play	playing
helped	help	helping
jumped	jump	jumping
growled	growl	growling
licked	lick	licking
pushed	push	pushing
talked	talk	talking
worked	work	working
rowed	row	rowing
crashed	crash	crashing
cried	cry	crying
hurried	hurry	hurrying

1. The ice cream was **melting** in the sun.
2. It is **snowing** and the ground is turning white.
3. I was **pumping** up the tyres on my bike.
4. I am not well, so I am **staying** in bed today.
5. The ambulance was **rushing** to the car crash.
6. I have lost my necklace and we are **looking** everywhere for it.
7. I was **locking** the back door with a key when it broke.
8. I was **washing** my mum's car when I got my clothes wet.
9. On Saturdays I like staying up late and **watching** TV.
10. It is the end of the race and I am **slowing** down because I am tired.

■ PAGE 48

yawning   playing   hurrying
jumping   crying   trying
punching   mowing   carrying
washing   rowing   crying
missing   showing   spying

■ PAGE 49

1. stopping   6. chasing
2. patting   7. dancing
3. scrubbing   8. nudging
4. flapping   9. wiggling
5. begging   10. liking

■ PAGE 50

1. hop hopped hopping
2. race raced racing
3. cry cried crying
4. wave waved waving
5. pray prayed praying
6. snow snowed snowing
7. kick kicked kicking
8. stop stopped stopping
9. scrub scrubbed scrubbing
10. push pushed pushing

■ PAGE 51

Verb	Verb + ED	Verb + ING
play	played	playing
cry	cried	crying
show	showed	showing
bake	baked	baking
watch	watched	watching

■ PAGE 52

92   Phonics and Spelling 3

```
H  B  W  F  R  T  B  P  H
Y  Y  F  O  M  T  A  Z  D
R  N  W  O  J  L  R  L  H
F  O  O  T  S  T  E  P  S
P  T  T  B  K  K  F  L  M
Q  M  Z  A  H  L  O  N  Q
N  F  J  L  C  D  O  V  T
L  M  T  L  Y  X  T  X  N
F  O  O  T  P  R  I  N  T
```

1. spoon   2. brush   3. sun

■ PAGE 54

1. headache   4. headmistress
2. headlights   5. headphones
3. headmaster   6. headlines

1. YESTERDAY   5. DAYBREAK
2. TODAY   6. DAYLIGHT
3. DAYTIME   7. DAYDREAM
4. MONDAY

■ PAGE 55

dismiss
unfair
disagree
unhappy
discourage
unhealthy
unpopular
disapprove
unusual

1. UNCERTAIN   6. UNLIKE
2. DISCOVER   7. UNCOMMON
3. UNLOCK   8. UNPLEASANT
4. DISAGREE   9. DISHONEST
5. DISAPPEAR   10. DISEASE

■ PAGE 56

defeat   defend   delay   defer   deduce
refresh   reduce   refer
prepare   prefer   pretend

1. decay   defy   demand   depart   detective
2. recycle   replace   research   reverse   reward
3. precaution prefix   prepare   pretend   prevent

■ PAGE 57

1. My teacher **asked** me a tricky question.
2. I **whispered** to my sister, so that no one else could hear me.
3. The policeman was **shouting**, so that the crowd could hear him.
4. I put my hand up to **answer** the questions.
5. My aunty **screamed**, 'Get that mouse out of here!'
6. I **called** out to my friend across the street.
7. 'What a funny joke,' the man **laughed**.
8. My brother and I were **arguing** over who was the biggest.

1. roar   3. squeak
2. bark   4. hiss

5. 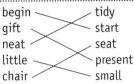 miaow   7. moo
6. bleat   8. quack

■ PAGE 58

1. speak   6. loud
2. home   7. right
3. dish   8. ocean
4. angry   9. sleepy
5. close   10. simple

begin ———— tidy
gift ⤬ start
neat ⤬ seat
little ⤬ present
chair ———— small

■ PAGE 59

1. sad   unhappy
2. sick   ill
3. end   finish
4. boat   ship
5. bag   case
6. rug   mat
7. bug   insect

■ PAGE 60

Words that rhyme with...					
atch	itch	etch	otch	utch	teach
catch	ditch	fetch	notch	hutch	each
patch	hitch	sketch	blotch	dutch	speech
latch					

1. witch   4. hutch
2. stretch   5. notch
3. scratch

■ PAGE 61

1. peach   4. patch
2. pitch   5. screech
3. watch

bu**tch**er   ki**tch**en   ma**tch**stick   sti**tch**es   hopsco**tch**

```
Q  B  U  T  C  H  E  R  J  E  U  O
M  N  Y  K  I  T  C  H  E  N  H  B
W  S  T  I  T  C  H  E  S  F  G  S
L  M  A  T  C  H  S  T  I  C  K  Z
H  O  P  S  C  O  T  C  H  R  D  K
```

■ PAGE 62

sledge
fudge
bridge
fridge
hedge
badger

1. dedge   2. bidge   3. widge

■ PAGE 63

1. badge   4. judge
2. ledge   5. nudge
3. edge

smudge – judge
ledge – sledge
fridge – bridge

■ PAGE 64

K with a hard C		Silent K	
kiln	kick	knead	knock
keep	kerb	kneel	knot
kind	kite	knife	knack
	kilt		

1. kangaroo
2. keyhole
3. kiss
4. kick
5. kayak
6. kill
7. kilogram
8. koala

■ PAGE 65

1 KEY
2 KITE
3 KETTLE
4 KITCHEN
5 KENNEL
6 KING

Secret word - Kitten

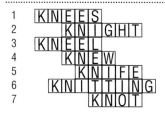

1 KNEES
2 KNIGHT
3 KNEEL
4 KNEW
5 KNIFE
6 KNITTING
7 KNOT

Secret words - Silent K

Alphabetical order – kennel kettle key king kitchen kite
kneel knees knew knife knight knitting knot

■ PAGE 66

1. I had to clean my shoes because they were **dirty**.
2. The pizza was very **tasty** and I ate it all.
3. The **funny** clown made us laugh.
4. The porridge was cold and **lumpy**.
5. The jelly hadn't set and it was still **runny**.
6. The monster was big and **hairy**.
7. The garden is **grassy** and green.
8. My cat's dinner smells **fishy**.

stripy lucky sandy rusty smelly

■ PAGE 67

1. cloudy   4. sunny
2. windy   5. rainy
3. foggy

1. sunny – funny   4. batty – chatty
2. gusty – dusty   5. foggy – boggy
3. chilly – silly   6. spicy – icy

■ PAGE 68

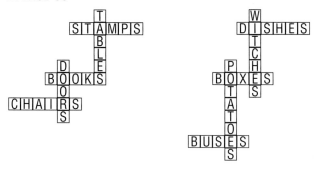

■ PAGE 69

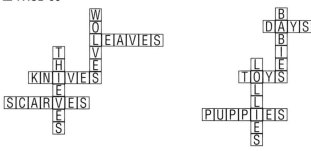

■ PAGE 70

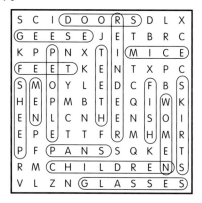

■ PAGE 71

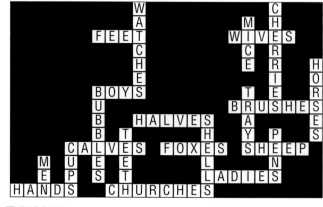

■ PAGE 72

kneel   **k**nit
gnat   **w**reck
wrong   **wh**isper
wheel

94   Phonics and Spelling 3

■ PAGE 73

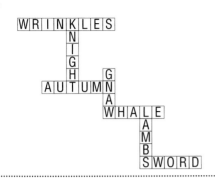

■ PAGE 74

1. spaceship
2. toothbrush
3. crossroads
4. tablecloth
5. windmill
6. rainbow
7. jellyfish
8. bedroom
9. thunderstorm
10. newspaper

■ PAGE 75

1. The **doorbell** rang.
2. It is much easier to run **downhill**.
3. I love **strawberries** and cream.
4. The witch flew away on her **broomstick**.
5. I sat down in the **armchair**.
6. There are swings in the **playground**.

torch – flashlight
all – everyone
astronaut – spaceman
pavement – footpath
road – highway

■ PAGE 76

1. The quiet cat purred **quietly**.
2. The neat children wrote **neatly**.
3. The nervous driver drove **nervously**.
4. The shy girl smiled **shyly**.
5. The quick runner ran **quickly**.
6. The kind nurse treated people **kindly**.
7. The nice lady spoke **nicely**.
8. The bold puppy barked **boldly**.
9. The loud teenager yelled **loudly**.
10. The sweet bird san **sweetly**.

happily
funnily
noisily
lazily
prettily

■ PAGE 77

■ PAGE 78

1. A cat is **smaller** than a horse and a mouse is the **smallest** of the three.
2. The boy who came second was **happier** than the boy who came last, but the winner was the **happiest**.
3. I think a cat is **braver** than a mouse but a lion is the **bravest**.
4. My mum is **older** than me and my grandma is the **oldest**.
5. My twin sister is **sillier** than me, but my little brother is the **silliest**.
6. My desk is **neater** than my friend's, but she says hers is the **neatest**.

faster — thinner
shortest — youngest
wider — slower
easier — prettiest
oldest — longest
ugliest — richer
poorer — harder

■ PAGE 79

faster	fastest
darker	darkest
taller	tallest

hotter	hottest
fitter	fittest
bigger	biggest

slower	slowest
neater	neatest
weaker	weakest

safer	safest
later	latest
nicer	nicest

happier	happiest
baggier	baggiest
funnier	funniest

■ PAGE 80

FUL	LESS
painful	spotless
useful	toothless
cheerful	careless
tearful	harmless

■ PAGE 81

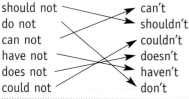

should not → shouldn't
do not → don't
can not → can't
have not → haven't
does not → doesn't
could not → couldn't

I am → I'm
we are → we're
you are → you're
they are → they're

we will → we'll
I will → I'll
she will → she'll
they will → they'll
he will → he'll

1. don't
2. you're
3. we're
4. haven't
5. doesn't
6. they're
7. she'll
8. can't

■ PAGE 82

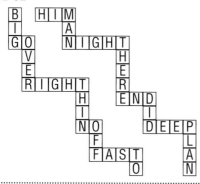

```
B H I M
I   A
G O   N I G H T
V       H
E       E
R I G H T   R
    H   E N D
    I     I
    N   D E E P
    O       L
  F A S T   A
      O     N
```

1. down
2. even
3. wet
4. happy
5. out
6. ugly
7. best
8. full
9. old
10. last

■ PAGE 83

1. another at away
2. car children cry
3. dad did door
4. last left look
5. name next now
6. past pig play

```
B A N K
B E G I N
B I S C U I T
B R E A D
C L A W
C O O K
D A R K
D R I N K
```

hidden message: nice work

```
G R E W
H A V E
H E L P
L I T T L E
M A D E
M O T H E R
W E N T
W H E N
```

hidden message: well done

■ PAGE 84

1. My baby sister talks **nonsense**.
2. I like **non-fiction** books about animals.
3. **Non-stick** saucepans are easy to clean.
4. My teacher says we should **co-operate** and get on together.
5. We are learning about maps and **combine**.
6. To make cakes you have to **combine** eggs, butter, sugar and flour.
7. In winter we use **antifreeze** to stop our car freezing up.
8. My doctor gave me **antibiotics** when I was ill.
9. The clock was broken and the hands were going around **anticlockwise**.
10. My friend and I wanted to **explore** the caves.
11. I am **excited** about my birthday party next week.
12. Healthy food and **exercise** will make you fit.

■ PAGE 85

1. He jumps over the **waves** at the beach.
   He **waves** goodbye to his dad.
2. My **watch** helps me tell the time.
   I like to **watch** cartoons on TV.
3. I threw a **stick** for my dog to chase.
   I use glue to **stick** things.
4. I washed the dishes in the **sink**.
   The old boat began to **sink**.

```
L I G H T
P O S T
M A T C H
B O O T
N A I L S
P L A Y
M I N E
S P R I N G
```

■ PAGE 86

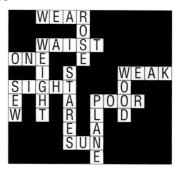

```
W E A R
O
W A I S T
O N E   S
E
S I G H T   W E A K
E     A   O
W     R P O O R
      E L D
      S A
      U N
      E
```